GRACE IN FREEDOM

KARL RAHNER

GRACE IN FREEDOM

HERDER AND HERDER

1969
Herder and Herder
232 Madison Avenue
New York, N. Y. 10016

Burns & Oates Ltd.
25 Ashley Place
London S. W. 1

Original edition:
"Gnade als Freiheit: Kleine theologische Beiträge",
Herder, Freiburg, 1968

Translated and adapted by:
Hilda Graef

Library of Congress Catalog Card Number: 78–85969
First Published in West Germany © 1969 Herder KG
Printed in West Germany by Herder

CONTENTS

III. RELIGIOUS PATTERNS

IV. ECUMENICAL PERSPECTIVES

V. FREE ACCEPTANCE OF CREATURLINESS AND CROSS

VI. COMMITMENT TO THE CHURCH AND PERSONAL FREEDOM

I. RESPONSIBILITY IN THE POST-CONCILIAR CHURCH

The Christians' Responsibility for the Church after the Council

I should like to discuss first the ancient tradition which is also the very latest, secondly the transition period which is now beginning, thirdly the cooperation demanded of the laity, and fourthly something which must always be there and which is most important also in this context, namely the patience of life.

I

If I say first something about the old things that remain and yet are always the latest, I hope I shall not be regarded as a reactionary who intensely dislikes the whole Council and the movement that has originated from it, and who refrains from criticizing this whole mentality only from a certain *esprit de corps*. This is not so. For I was also somehow involved in the Council, even though I did not have very much say, and I regard its spirit and its decrees as very important, especially for the Church of the future. Nevertheless, in my opinion our first duty after the Council is to be faithful to the old which is also the new. People who do not know very much about their Catholic faith and journalists who are always after novelties have discussed the Council mostly from the point of view of new and revolutionary developments. Some proclaimed that the Council had produced a revolution in the Church, others regretted the innovations or thought they had not gone far enough. In a word, the Council was judged from a point of view that could not be the final and decisive one. What is decisive for the Church and hence also for us Catholics is the ancient teaching, because it is fundamentally ever-new, for it is what decides our life, our salvation, our eternal future and our situation before the judgment seat of God. For the latest is precisely the holy, Christian Catholic faith which we have received as children, and which we have preserved in our life, perhaps even through many troubles and difficulties, our active Catholic faith of which we shall have to give an account before God; and this faith, of course, remains the same.

Only those who have no understanding of the Church and of Christianity could imagine that the Council was in danger of changing anything of the Catholic dogma, or, on the other hand, that it ought to have done so. This is complete nonsense, and this inheritance, transmitted to us by Jesus Christ through the apostles, has never for a moment been in danger of being doubted or changed by the Council. Of course, we are historical men, placed by God in a definite historical situation; hence we shall always have to see the eternal truth, which is Jesus Christ, under new perspectives, and thus this faith does not remain a sum of dead formulae but is a truly living faith. It is the faith of the Church such as it has always been, faith in the triune God, in Jesus Christ our Lord and Saviour, in our duty in this life, in the judgment, in the grace of God which, through Jesus Christ, forgives, saves, sanctifies and ultimately even deifies our life. The Council has changed nothing in this constant faith. For this faith can never change. And thus we live both before and after the Council by that ultimate, mysterious and yet so obvious substance of our faith, that is in living union with the holy and eternal God, who is not only our Creator and Lord because he has called us his creatures forth from nothingness, but who is also eternal love, who gives us his own glorious eternal life in Jesus Christ and his Spirit. This is the old faith, just as the last problems of our life remain the old ones: that we should become loving and unselfish, that we should bear the darknesses of existence, that we should finally come to terms with death, that we should do our duty also when we can expect no earthly reward, that we should follow our crucified Lord and Saviour. This remains our task also after the Council, just as our faith remains the same. And this includes also the ultimate moral principles of our life and the divine law of the Church which is given by revelation. Of course, there is and must be much human law in the Church, and this can be changed; indeed, it not only may but must be adapted to new circumstances. Nevertheless, there is also an immutable law of the Church. Through his religious education every mature Christian ought to be able to distinguish between the actual dogma of the Church and theological opinions that may be changed and improved, between immutable divine law and changeable human law. To give an example: The Church may change and adapt to modern life certain principles of her human law according to which a Catholic must marry; but only a person of little theological knowledge would draw the conclusion that the Church could ever abolish the indissolubility of the sacramental consummated marriage if only there were enough protests. This would be silly; for the one thing belongs to the human law of the Church, the other to the demands Christ himself makes on us. Thus the ancient laws and doctrines which remain ever new are contained also in what we have learned in our youth about the life of piety, the Christian family life and the Christian upbringing of children. Here, too, it is not the case that suddenly all the good things of the past are no longer valid and that everything has to be changed. Of course, we all live in an era of transition, of greater and quicker changes. We shall speak of this presently. Hence everyone has, of course, the duty to transform and renew from their very roots all these inherited traditions of Christian life, piety and education according to modern needs. Nevertheless, today, too, a Christian must continue to pray and to remain in living contact with his God through the spirit of grace. He cannot simply live in the commotion of his job, of keeping up with the Joneses and the rat race, with no thought for his true and eternal vocation. And, even though it is very difficult in our pluralistic society, it is nevertheless the duty of Christian parents to transmit to their children the sacred inheritance of the Christian faith and also of a Christian life provided with practical guiding lines. They will not be asked by God whether and to what extent they have succeeded in individual cases, but they will certainly be asked whether they have done all they could to transmit to their children this Christian inheritance by a really generous Christian life and example. Thus faith is immutable divine law of the Church and also true and living practice, determined not only by abstract principles but also by concrete ideals. It is Christian life at risk, the old religion which will always be new. Christians certainly cannot be dispensed from the duty to hold in high esteem the ancient faith, not even by a modern Council, though this had to speak mostly of other things, precisely because the basic doctrines could be presupposed. Indeed, such novel ideas never entered the head of any Council father.

II

We are living in a time of transition in which the future has, as it were, already begun. Technological, social and economic factors enforce all kinds of innovations and changes in all departments of life at a tremendous and ever-increasing pace. In such a time the Church cannot simply pretend to have nothing else to do but to remain as she was before and as older people have known her in their younger years. Of course, there are those among us who would like the Church to remain a refuge, a backwater of history into which they can retire because they are afraid of the pace of historical development and all the change and insecurity this entails. The Church has clearly said through the Council that she does not want to live in the backwater of our history. True, there has also been much pettiness at the Council as well as exaggerated caution in some respects and hesitations between conservative and progressive attitudes. Nevertheless, the Church has there stated unequivocally that she must serve men and will courageously take upon herself all the risks of this service and enter the changing history of our time.

There is, of course, a great deal that is controversial. Whether or not the liturgy to which we have been used from childhood is more beautiful than the new one, whether new rules, for example about mixed marriages or denominational schools, are acceptable or not—such questions will be answered differently whether one is "conservative" or "progressive". Some may find these rules too modern or useless, others even too conservative. But we Catholics are living in an actual Church and not in a cloud cuckooland of abstract ideals, hence we must bear with her when she is trying to confront our time cautiosly, yet with courage. For we should certainly be attached to the old ways, but also have courage to approach what is new and as yet untried and thus bear with the uncertainties of a transition period.

The present situation in the Church may be compared to a college with a new president who has new ideas on education and other subjects. In such a case some students will probably be relieved that the authorities have at last seen the light, while others, used to the old style, may first abuse their newly found freedom. Then the old people will say that this is what happens if one abandons the old, well-tried discipline and goes in for new experiments. For in such a transition period those who could really cope with the new situation do not yet exist, because they were prevented from doing so by the old style; hence at first things become worse rather than better. Ten or twenty years ago a seminary, for example, still worked very well in the old way. Everyone knew what he had to do; if anyone did not obey he was expelled, and thus the whole outfit ran smoothly. But now there is a new situation, and lo and behold, on the one hand one realizes that there must be changes, on the other everything appears to get only worse. But this always happens, and it must happen also in the Church, indeed we cannot expect anything else. One will grumble that he must constantly be bobbing up and down at Mass, that there are even more sermons than before and that they are therefore getting worse, while the other will say that this is nothing to worry about, because we cannot yet have made much progress.

We must simply realize that God has placed us in a Church which is in a state of transition. We are members of this Church, and while loving what is permanent yet ever new, we must also have sufficient courage, patience and generosity to give a real chance to what is new and not to destroy it in advance by inner and outer resistance and constant nagging criticism.

In such a situation we have the inescapable duty to endure the uncertainties of such a transition period. We must not be defeatist and cry that the whole Church is heading for disaster, but neither should we have the childish idea of a crazy *avant-garde* that the Church should move ever faster, that what has been achieved is nothing and that everything that is new in the Church is but a modest beginning leading to unheard-of things. For these people all the decisions of the Council are already out of date and uninteresting. But we must remember that our Church is a Church of the whole world. Failure to understand this shows a provincial mentality which has not yet grasped that we are living in a period of world history when no country can any longer be self-sufficient whether in the economic, cultural, scientific or social spheres. In such a period it would be childish to judge the Church and her policies only according to the needs of a particular country or province. We are children of the one Church despite all pluralism which can also exist in the Church, and despite the pluralism of the Churches which was also recognized by Vatican II, despite, also, the decentralization, for example, through the bishops' conferences. And because we live, and want to live, in a world-wide Church, we must bear with a certain self-criticism that which is inevitable if the Church is not to disintegrate into particular Churches which no longer have a common life. To say it again, we must endure the period of transition which is now beginning with devotion to what is old and courage with regard to the new, bearing with insecurity, pain and experiments, all of which is simply inevitable.

III

We are not merely Christians who find ourselves members of the Catholic Church. We are determined to be such. One idea especially has penetrated through the considerable clericalism that existed in the Catholic Church. It was this, that the Church does not only consist of the clergy, that is the Pope, the bishops and the priests, organized to look after the eternal salvation of others, but that we all, baptized Catholics, are the Church. This means that, despite all justified, even necessary criticism of the Church, the behaviour of her ministers and so forth, we must nevertheless always realize that we ourselves are this Church.

It is said, not without reason, that a nation has usually the government it deserves, that the government actually reflects the whole people. In spite of certain flaws this principle is, on the whole, quite correct.

It is more or less the same with the Church. For it is not true that only the most stupid, narrow-minded and clerical men rise to the highest ecclesiastical offices, so that a generous, holy and idealistic people would have a wholly unworthy clergy. No, what is generally seen in the clergy is also to be found in the laity: inadequacy, shortsightedness, ineffectual good will, fear or blind *avant-gardism*. We ought really to make our own, even to the very marrow, the fundamental concept of Vatican II, namely that we ourselves are the Church. As a result every right to criticize, to care, to cooperate, to object, warn and protest must not come from outside but from within, from a member who is truly conscious of his own responsibility as well as of his own inadequacy.

After the Council such cooperation, which is the right and duty of every baptized Christian, must first take the form of a personal study and understanding of the Council decrees. Actually all of them are of some interest to every-body. Here I cannot, of course, discuss the contents of these decrees, but I should only like to draw attention to one thought from the Constitution on the Church: The Church is the holy people of God seeking eternal life through the sufferings and the wilderness of this time, and we are this Church. Hence the Church is a Church of sinners, an inadequate Church which must continue to learn throughout her history. She is not only the objective institute of salvation which confronts me and to whose authority I concede certain things but towards which I am, on the whole, in a defensive position. Much would be gained if we were to learn this one thing from the Con-stitution on the Church, namely that not only we are, but actually I am the Church. For I really cannot expect a Church that would be different from myself, the in-adequate sinner who must constantly rebuild his life through a thousand byways and experiences.

We should further learn from the same Constitution that the Church really does not teach a two-tier theory of her members, according to which some would trot along the common road, hoping nevertheless to arrive at God, while the others, priests and religious, constituting as it were the aristocracy, walk in more exalted paths. We should learn from this Decree that every Christian is called to the perfect love of God in his own way, even if he must realize it through his secular life in the world. For the spirit of the evangelical counsels, of the Sermon on the Mount, of the cross, the spirit of hope in the risen Christ and an eschatological attitude to life belong to all Christian existence and are binding on all.

There is also a special Decree on the Apostolate of the Laity, and one on the Missions in which the Church tells Christians—that is herself—that in the age of declining colonialism and Europeanism, too, the missions have a permanent duty also in the non-Western countries for which every Christian is responsible in his own way.

Then there is the Decree on Ecumenism, and the Declaration on non-Christian Religions with its condemnation of antisemitism which has not yet been destroyed everywhere. There is also the Pastoral Constitution on the Church in the Modern World. This is truly a pastoral constitution, which can really fire the curiosity of laymen, because here the Church is trying to confront the burning questions of our time in a provisional manner, it is true, but nevertheless in a suitable way.

In the documents on bishops, priests, etc., there are also passages which should be of interest to laymen. This is especially true of the texts dealing with the conception of the Church's ministry as a service, which is not meant to eliminate the task of the laymen. For these are not regarded as merely passive objects of the saving activities of the ministry, but, on the basis of true Christian equality and freedom as collaborators of the hierarchy, so that actually the hierarchy must only serve the Christian life which is to be realized by the laity. I should like to illustrate this by a comparison, though this is not to be found in any Council document. In a chess club, too, the main thing is that chess should be played well, and that masters of the game should be trained there. Everything else, the functionaries, the cash registers, the president, the club meetings and statutes are, indeed, necessary and cannot be abolished; but their true meaning is to serve playing chess. The true stars of a chess club are the best players, not the cashier or the president who may, indeed, be players who have failed. Exactly the same is the case in the Catholic Church (and this is not an avantgardist idea of mine). All presiding ministers of the Church, from the Pope and

the bishops down to the parish priests and chaplains, exist
only so that there may be Christians, that is men and
women who believe, hope and love, who bear their cross,
who see light even in darkness, who firmly hope even
against hope, men who have the folly and the courage to
love in a loveless world. All sermons, all papal decrees, all
canon law, all sacred congregations in Rome, all bishops—
in short the whole organization of the Church exists only
to assist the true Christian life in the hearts of men. Where
this meaning is lost it becomes only man's ridiculous
presumption before God.

The true lights of the Church, those who are most important for the eternal salvation of mankind as well as of
individuals are not the Pope, the bishops or the cardinals
in their red cassocks, but those who possess and radiate
most faith, hope and love, most humility and unselfishness,
most fortitude in carrying the cross, most happiness and
confidence. If a Pope does all this as well or perhaps even
better than, for example, John XXIII, well, then he is not
only a Pope but a wonderful Christian, then it happens that,
if I may say so, the president of the chess club is for once
also himself a great chess player. But this would be a happy
coincidence which God is not bound to bring about and
which he has not guaranteed. If we are looking at the
Church in this way, we shall not find it difficult to accept
that the cashier is responsible for the finances and the president of this holy society directs its activities. But we ought
to remain conscious of what is both our pride and our
burden, namely that the Church depends ultimately on
ourselves.

But I have strayed rather far from my subject. We ought
also to think of the Declaration on Religious Freedom, of
the Constitution on the Liturgy, the Declaration on Christian Education, the Decree on the Instruments of Social

Communication, to name a few more of the Council documents. For all these contain also matters of concern to the laity, even though perhaps stated imperfectly and in a way which might have been done better by a more competent layman.

Hence the first thing necessary for lay cooperation is an understanding of, and interest in, the decrees of the Council.

The second is the true lay apostolate which has to be exercised in one's ordinary life. There is certainly also a very praiseworthy and important lay apostolate which consists in the direct cooperation with the hierarchy in the most diverse spheres. This has also been emphasized by the Decree on the Apostolate of the Laity. Far be it from me to belittle the importance of such an apostolate. Nevertheless it remains true, indeed it is of decisive importance, that the most essential lay apostolate consists in the fulfilment of one's family, professional, and of course also one's civic duties. At first sight this apostolate in a secular world may seem to have nothing to do with religion and be the same task as everybody else's; nevertheless it is the layman's principal duty after the Council, as it had been before.

There is no need to affix a particularly pious label to these seemingly so secular duties of family and professional life with all their daily bitterness and boredom, and to the civic duties from which no one should try to escape. We need not adorn this reality with pious sighs or a complicated theological ideology. Life itself will lead the layman into depths which are actually basic Christian situations, whether they are interpreted as such or not, whose darkness is illumined by the light of the gospel and which can be borne only with the help of God's grace.

Art. 7 of the Decree on the Missions says in so many words that God can give in ways known to himself the grace of faith and thus the hope and love necessary for eternal life also to those whom the actual message of the gospel has not reached. But this does not dispense Catholics from belonging to the Church or authorize them to become anonymous Christians themselves. Catholic laymen must take up their place in life and face their family, their love, their children (who perhaps do not always come up to their expectations), their professional duties which grow ever more irksome and their duties as citizens; in doing so they will meet situations in which, because they reflect on their faith, they will know how to behave as Christians living in the grace of God, the light of the gospel and the imitation of the crucified Christ. This is their true and ultimate apostolate. Such a life will radiate, perhaps precisely because there is no pious talk. Though this is not meant to imply that an educated layman ought not also sometimes have the courage, in the right place and in the right manner, to give an account of the hope that is in him and, as the apostle says, is active in his life.

The third element which belongs to this cooperation and which must be emphasized may be connected with art. 26 of the Constitution on the Church. For this speaks of the local churches as the place where the presence of the Church as such is actualized in the highest form. For there a concrete community is gathered round the altar, there the death and resurrection of the Lord are announced in his gospel, there the congregation knows itself to be united as the body of Christ and thus as a brotherly community of those who love one another. And there, according to the Constitution, the Church is truly present. Now it seems to me that after the Council this experience and piety of the Church is demanded more intensely from us than may have been the case before. I have no illusions about the modern local church, that is to say the parish such as it exists today. But we can no longer treat the Church with her buildings and ministers, her doctrine and sacraments as a kind of religious department store in which we buy the things that are necessary for our personal salvation. We cannot regard the other Christians simply as customers buying, indeed in the same store, but otherwise quite uninteresting to us. For the Church is not simply an institution for the private religious needs of the individual.

The Church is the holy people of God existing in this shabby parish with this parish priest such as he is, though he may preach bad sermons and I may, in ordinary life, often quarrel with these boring creatures, Tom, Dick and Harry, who gather in this church. This church must not only be patiently borne because unfortunately I cannot shop at this spiritual store at an hour when everyone else is excluded. For this local church is the place where the layman must really find his place and his responsibility, where he must feel at home, just as in a family where one also does not like everyone.

I know that parishes such as they should be are few and far between, I am also quite willing to concede to the educated layman the right to satisfy his essential religious needs outside the parish to which he accidentally belongs —indeed, canon law does the same. But if these local communities in which the Church appears are not yet ideal, we ought not to say uncharitably: I will wait till things are better and then I will join the parish. No, it is our duty to do as much as we can to make sure that the Church in which the death and resurrection of the Lord are celebrated really comes into existence, for we are called to fashion her.

This collaboration also involves the dialogue with the Church authorities. Just as in the chess club, somebody must also have the last word in the Church. It is a sign of maturity if a person leaves the final decision to another and submits to it even if, rightly or wrongly, he does not consider it a wise decision. But the Church herself wants a fraternal dialogue between laymen and the authorities, because she knows that, though not everyone in the Church is called to the sacramental ministry, all Christians are members of the royal priesthood and this is ultimately the higher order. For, to repeat what has been said before, the importance of the Church's ministry corresponds to the measure of faith, hope and charity which it produces. Even a Pope is judged by God according to the humility, the love, the faithfulness, the faith and hope he has practised in the exercise of his office.

For this reason the authorities of the Church can really seek a dialogue with all Christians who form the Church and have a share in her royal priesthood. It would certainly be a good thing if there were more, perhaps even institutional, possibilities available for such a dialogue. But unless laymen themselves patiently seek such a dialogue with their parish priests, their bishops and so forth, it will not happen.

A last point I want to make about this collaboration is the necessity to endure the situation of the diaspora.

I do not here mean the diaspora in which Protestants and Catholics live together. What I mean is the religiously atomized pluralistic society of our time of which all forms of Christianity are only a part and in which we live together with post-Christian neo-pagans, if I may be allowed to use this expression. Much could be said about the right understanding of this diaspora situation, but I cannot do this here. I should only like to mention this problem and to bring it to the attention of my readers, recommending it to their meditation with regard to their own Christian experience.

IV

I should like finally to say something about the "patience of life". St. Paul once mentioned the "hypomone", the endurance of hope. Today man is more than ever responsible for himself. True, on the one hand the individual's sphere of freedom seems to be, and actually is, restricted by social and cultural conditions. But on the other he has immense chances to shape his life; in fact, man can do incredibly much. He is, as it were, no longer bound and supported by society and the ideological situation of his life. He must have an inner centre, a structural principle of his life if he is not to disintegrate under the pluralistic tensions from outside.

In this situation one can do much, but not everything at once, and so there comes about a new kind of being disappointed in life. True, in former times life was often very narrow, as regards one's profession and marriage as well as the education of children and political and cultural activities. The man in the street had few possibilities, but by this very fact he was as it were held together from outside, he was confronted with a certain structure and shape of his life from the beginning, so that he did not need to think very much about it. Marriage was stable, even if outwardly rather than inwardly. But it was stable nevertheless. But now man finds himself in a situation in which he can do all sorts of things, but has, of course, to choose among all these many possibilities, since life must retain a certain inner unity and consistency. Thus he must go without many things, which he had to do also in former times, but then he was not actually aware of it. Thus our contemporaries begin to suffer from an inner disappointment, an irritation that was impossible in former times because the whole life was different from what it is today.

Today we are perhaps more disappointed in life than former generations, and the repeated upheavals in the life
of society and of individuals may be explained by this
mood of despair, because there is so much colourless boredom in life despite its great possibilities. But all this means
a new duty for the Christian: he must bear it patiently and
not imagine that it could be overcome by sexual promis-
cuity, incessant activity, moneymaking, a never ending
round of pleasure, tourism and whatever other means
there are to drown the ultimate *Angst* of life. We Christians must endure the disappointment of life in faith and
hope, in living personal prayer to God in the grace of
Christ, and in willingly suffering all this misery. This may
perhaps sound strange, but it seems to me that this is a
decisive factor of our Christian life today. For only thus
can we face the judgment of God and bear witness to our
Christian faith before the world.

We must be able to be resigned, to bear this diffused
misery of our life without going mad, to say it bluntly, as
long as it is still day and as long as we live; we must not
imagine that we ought to be only happy in our job, that
our children must do well, that our marriage must be
nothing but bliss and security; we must bear with the feel-
ing that we are paying more into the bank of life, as it
were, than we get out of it. For we begin to be Christians living in the grace of God only if we are honest even when it
is no longer the best policy, and we exercise our true apostolate precisely when we appear to be stupid and without
much social prestige. But we can really do this only if we
slowly begin to believe from the very centre of our heart
in God, in Jesus Christ, in his grace, and in eternal life.
Thus the last is once more the ancient constant faith which
is also the most new: God, Jesus Christ, his grace, his
forgiveness and eternal life. If we truly live from this

centre, but otherwise live in the modern way, even, let us say, with a Jaguar, but really as Christians, then, it seems to me, we have done what the Council expects us to do. For the whole apparatus and the paperwork of the Council did and could not want to produce anything but faith, hope and love. This is both the easiest and the most difficult, for it is the holy art of living as Christians in the grace of God.

Advice to a Worried Catholic

The Council is over. There are not a few truly pious Catholics even in the highest echelons of the clergy who are under the torturing impression that the Council has brought the Church nothing but disquiet and insecurity, a false desire for novelty and silly chatter, even a threat to the true faith. A symptom of this attitude is the group that calls itself *Una Voce* and which wants especially, though not only, to preserve the Latin liturgy: it corresponds to the Latin Mass Society in England and other similar organizations in other countries. There is another symptom: a Bavarian abbot said some time ago, probably not quite seriously, but nevertheless from his tormented heart: This Council is of the devil. Now this is certainly not true. But we must ask ourselves how to answer such irritated and troubled Catholics.

There are many Catholic priests and laymen who are not at all, or at least much less worried. They regard the Council as a wonderful event, brought about by the Spirit, a new beginning in the Church. Now all these who feel themselves as avantgardists or at least want to be regarded as such ought to take the other, worried Catholics quite seriously. We are all brothers in the one Church of the same faith and the same love which unite us. We should treat each other as such, but we find this difficult, because we are sinful, self-opinionated and presumptuous human beings. Nevertheless we must always try again. Now, after the Council, the so-called progressives have no right at all to treat their "conservative" brothers und sisters in the same way as they themselves, rightly or wrongly, thought they had been treated by their so-called opponents before the Council. Now the progressives must show that *they* can be charitable, generous and tolerant.

Futhermore, not everything that is worrying conservative Catholics after the Council is only the imagination of old-fashioned people who confuse traditional customs with ever-valid truths. In the liturgy as well as in other departments of the Church's life there are regrettable excrescences and an arbitrary desire for novelties which must be repressed courageously and charitably. Hence such conservative people, too, have a genuine individual function and duty in the whole Church, provided only that they are obedient to the authorities, open to their directives and loving and reasonable towards all their brethren. No one can identify only himself with the Church and her authentic life; everyone has only his own particular gift which he may and should incorporate in the Church, even though this is impossible without a certain fraternal controversy. This plurality of gifts which may at times combat each other will not destroy the unity of faith and love in the one Church. This is guaranteed by the assistance of the Spirit and must be brought about by the authorities with which all must remain united in humility and love.

But within this framework the conservatives should realize their own particular gift quietly and courageously. They have the right to prevent the Latin liturgy from disappearing. Their instinct of faith should ask whether some new thesis of a theologian is still Christian and Catholic, whether it corresponds to the binding dogma pro-

claimed by the magisterium. They have the right to turn to
their bishops questioningly, complainingly, even accusing-
ly if they are justly scandalized in their conscience by what
they see, hear and otherwise experience in the Church. But
all this on condition that they are themselves charitable
and tolerant, prepared not to give up the dialogue with
their brothers who are of a different opinion. They must
not make mountains out of molehills and exaggerate
inevitable teething troubles into frightful catastrophes, but
bear patiently the all-too-human side of the Church to
which they, too, make their contribution.

Such worried Catholics must also be told this: it is
simply not true that everything has become uncertain
because of the Council. A so-called conservative cannot
be a true Catholic if he did, indeed, love the pre-conciliar
Church and her way of life, experienced her as the rock
of truth, but now can suddenly only protest against this
most recent Council and distrust its teaching and directives. True, this Council is just as human and contemporary
as all other Councils, but it is a Council of holy Church
and under the power of the Holy Spirit. But Catholics
must not obstinately oppose it only because they are not
used to its teaching and directives. For if they did they
would act like the Old Catholics after the First Vatican
Council, even if they do not officially leave the Church. For
the Old Catholics, too, did not want to admit that what
was new was only the present divinely willed historical
form of the old which they, too, thought they ought to
defend against a Church devoted to novelties. Such
worried Catholics who are already going wild even when
they have only to get up and sit down at Mass should really
ask themselves quite simply and charitably: What has become different in the Church and what has remained the
same? If they are true believers and not riding some partic-

ular hobby horse they must surely say that everything has remained the same that is really necessary for life as well as for death: the crucified and risen Christ, his grace, baptism, the true body and blood of the Lord in the Eucharist, the forgiveness of sins, the expectation of eternal life, the ancient dogma binding on all, the one commandment of the love of God and our neighbour. Is that so little? No, this is what really matters, and all this has remained because it is what is old and also only truly new.

Of course, there are new questions in dogmatic and moral theology, which have been discussed more openly at and after the Council and which have not yet been solved, among them questions of great importance also for the practical life. But this is not surprising, for the same has happened before, even if some conservative Christians did not realize it. It is, for example, a very grave question as to what exactly the proper Christian attitude towards atomic weapons is; the whole fate of humanity may hang on it. Yet even Pius XII could not give a definite answer. For there are darknesses in life which Christians and the Church have to bear with patience. These difficulties are laid on us by God, they have not been artificially produced by the malice of crazy theologians who will no longer accept anything. According to the will of God the Church that knows and makes decisions is also always the questioning and searching Church which must patiently endure this situation. Caution is not the same as cowardice. If the Church is cautious in questions of doctrine and discipline, perhaps even more so than in the past, if she waits for more information, carrying on a dialogue, perhaps even leaves much to the conscience of the individual, all this does not mean that the authorities have grown cowardly, they have not, for this reason, given up their responsibility and their power.

Finally, even in certain peripheral questions of theology, but especially in the liturgy, penitential discipline, administration and similar matters, there are no definite methods and hard and fast rules which would be wholly good and without any possible dangers. Hence there are theoretically unlimited pros and cons as regards possible decisions, and there will always also be good reasons against any particular decision. Such reasons have also existed against ancient and traditional decisions, even if they were not expressed in so many words and were not felt to be important by conservative people. Naturally such theoretical pros and cons exist also with regard to the decisions made or initiated by Vatican II. If a conservative Christian is against such a decision because he believes he has good reasons against it, these may perhaps be quite weighty and yet his protest against the decision may be unjustified. Every concrete decision stresses certain points in preference to others, though these, too, might have been emphasized. It is a matter of opinion which cannot be solved by discussion alone, but only by a decision which affirms one thing and abandons another, even if the latter was dear to many. Because the Church is universal she must often decide between many cultures, traditions, attitudes and tendencies, and in doing so may not please anyone completely, taking in too little that is new for one and retaining not enough of the old things for another. Certainly uniformity might frequently be abandoned and quite often this is actually done. But it is again a question of opinion whether something might be left open or whether it must be decided as binding for the whole Church. In the concrete case there will again be pros and cons about which the discussion might never end but which must be decided here and now.

This simple fact of human life as well as of the Church is often overlooked by the progressive, when he screams that developments are too slow, that antiquated habits and customs are not abandoned fast enough, especially with regard to canon law. But the worried conservative Catholic also falls into this same error if he thinks that everything must be preserved only because it is or was good. But the Church cannot move in all directions at once. A conservative Christian who only obstinately protests will sabotage the possible good effect of a new decision, and thus the new thing will be lost while the good old one is not really preserved. The brotherly dialogue between progressives and conservatives and of both with the authorities about how to deal with the situation of the future, this dialogue may and should continue. But it ought not to result in one party making impossible what is now right and good in the Church, for this could only lead to confusion. The conservative Catholic may well regret that a Latin High Mass is now very rare and he may well make use of his Christian freedom and choose a service which suits him. But if he attends a mass such as his own parish priest conducts he should attend to the essential of the mass, the ever-lasting sacrifice of Christ, which is present in every form of the eucharistic celebration and simply take part in this particular service.

The Church is the community of truth and love, and it is the same as in any other loving community of finite human beings: we must always love and accept one another also as men who are strangers to each other and who do not quite understand one another. For this is part of love and even of truth, in which we live only if we accept and endure also those whose personalities are alien or even incomprehensible to us. The Church is not meant to become an ever-decreasing little group of esoteric traditionalists which the world passes by, for this would mean betraying her mission, according to which she is not there for herself, but for men and the world. Therefore she must undergo the change that has begun at the Council. True, this may surprise and worry just some of her best members, while, on the other hand, she herself does not cease to remain unintelligible to outsiders, because her constant message still sounds foolish and scandalous. Today, however, her faithful members are asked whether they truly love the Church, accepting the change even though it appears strange at first, or whether by their secret or public protest they show that they have not really loved the Church herself, but only their idea of her. There have always been not only progressive, but also reactionary heresies and schisms in the Church. Today the conservatives in the Church are asked whether they will integrate their good gift of conservatism into the changing Church, or whether, in a latent heresy, they want to be reactionaries in the bad sense. This question does not imply a recipe for the solution of all actual questions, but it signalizes an attitude which is one of the decisive elements in the Church today.

To an Impatient Catholic

After the end of the Council there are now many impatient people who are disappointed. They had ardently and hopefully welcomed the Council, expecting that it would produce a Church which would convince the world because she would appear as the radiant bride of Christ, without spot or blemish. Yet now all seems to have remained more or less as it was before: theologians still struggle painfully with their problems, their is still a bureaucratic administration which seems to prefer the letter to the spirit, there is still no united Christendom, but we are still divided, fearing and mistrusting each other on both sides of the fence. We are still waiting for an obvious and effective reform of the curia, and brotherly collegiality in the Church is not much more than a fine word. The will of the clergy to give the laity a real share in the task and responsibility for the Church is still in its infancy, and the laymen themselves are not exactly wildly keen on it. The Church's responsibility for the world has not yet surpassed the most modest efforts, and the liturgical life seems to be a hybrid of old and new forms. The reform of canon law is still far away ... in short, there is nothing like a new Pentecost to be noticed, but rather quarrels and alienation among Catholics themselves, new unsolved questions in theology as well as in Christian living on which we had seemed to be agreed before the Council, the continuing silent apostasy of the masses, the rejection of faith, Christian morality and conviction in public life. Is not this sufficient reason for disappointment and especially for impatience? Are we not rightly impatient to see deeds following the beginnings made in the Council, theories changed into facts, principles into life? What can we say to the angry, impatient progressive Catholic now, after the Council?

First of all: there is, indeed, a justified and holy impatience, which has a right to make itself heard in the Church. Not everyone has every gift that is needed in the Church, and it is true that there need not be only angry and impatient Catholics. But they must also be there, because the Church needs them. We must on no account think that now the Church has got over the Council it is high time to restore peace and order as if, as an Italian Cardinal is supposed to have said, the Council had produced only broken pieces which would take a century to put together again. No, the Council was a beginning which must be continued. And for this purpose the Church needs a holy impatience, which should make itself heard in all legitimate ways. These ways include also those that do not please everyone and may not be comfortable for every bishop. This holy impatience must work like a driving motor: it may criticize and try to influence public opinion, it need not be afraid that every quarrel and every dispute it produces is a sign that it is unjustified or perverse. St. Paul, too, had his quarrels, even with Peter himself. And yet it was a holy and necessary quarrel. The peace of the Church is not the peace of a graveyard and has nothing to do with indifferent conformism.

But this impatience must truly be holy, unselfish, loving one's opponent as his brother and not scandalizing him wherever this can be avoided by generosity and love. This impatience must be humble, it must not imagine that God distributes his gifts in the Church in such a way that one party is wholly right and the other wholly wrong.

The impatient *theologians* must be told that they, too, must practise holy impatience. There are really incredibly many questions waiting to be clarified before theologians can assist those who preach the word of God in the way they expect. But even a new and living Catholic theology that does justice to modern man remains dependent on Catholic dogma and the teaching office of the Church. This theology does not want to be modern because it betrays the ancient faith or preaches another gospel that is no gospel. Of course, it is often difficult to decide whether, despite a man's good will, his efforts to understand better the gospel and the doctrine of the Church have really caused him to depart from the truth, or whether a traditionalist sold on the old formulae only thinks so. Of course, such an open question cannot be decided at the drop of a hat. But the orthodoxy of a Catholic theologian should not be suspect only because he does his duty honestly and weighing his own views, remaining in an open dialogue with the magisterium and prepared to leave the last word to the authorities of the Church, always lovingly adapting his individual understanding of the faith to that of the whole Church. He may well let his holy impatience become effective for the renewal of theology. But he should also know that his proper work is not to destroy traditional taboos but to build up an authentic, living faith.

Holy impatience has a difficult task in the Church. But this is quite natural, the Council will need a long time till it has more or less penetrated the various spheres of life. This was so in the case of earlier Councils, this is so also in the case of the last. The Council can only become effective through setbacks and hesitations, for it will often be difficult to know how to carry out ideal concepts in the sober sphere of reality. This is quite natural, but it is difficult to live with. It is even natural that at first a new concept is carried out less satisfactorily than an old one to which we are accustomed, that there will at first be a hybrid combination of the old and the new. There will be a mixed style which will really please nobody very much, hence holy impatience must be patient, it must hope against hope, it must hold its breath, resolutely yet tolerantly. These holy impatient people should realize that Rome was not built in a day, though the lazy and the reactionaries had better not pronounce these words. A Chinese proverb says that a man who is in a hurry must make a detour; this is certainly not always true, but sometimes it is quite applicable. Experiments and risks are certainly necessary in the Church today; there are many cases when dangerous ventures are demanded by a tutiorism properly understood. But if the Pope for example sometimes seems to apply the Chinese proverb, we should not at once accuse him of hesitation or even indecision. Popes, too, are finite human beings, influenced by their history and experience. Thus it is not always *a priori* certain that their actions and omissions are directly inspired by a superior wisdom. But the opposite cannot be presumed either. Nor should the impatient individual simply assume that his opinions and demands are definitely the voice of divine wisdom and the divine will. But even if the opinions and tendencies are not in harmony, the members of the Church, whether ministers or others, may yet be united in love and mutual respect, in the will to unity and the preservation of order, in the patience that bears with others. And it is part of an authentic Christianity that such virtues must always begin in oneself, even though they may be exploited by others.

Finally we must say something that may sound like defeatism but is not. The Church is and remains the pilgrim Church, the Church of sinners always needing a reform that can never end, she will never be a Church that will not cause us suffering. For we ourselves contribute to the sinfulness of the Church through our own misery. And this is true also of those who are impatient and full of holy zeal. Because their impatience is not always very holy, and so they resemble the man who wants to remove the speck in the other's eye but fails to notice the log in his own. For it remains true that we work most truly for a *holy* Church if we patiently and lovingly bear with the imperfect and unholy one, knowing full well that she ultimately shows forth only our own sinfulness. The true Catholic Christian gives the Church not only a limited advance of trust, love and patience. For he sees it ultimately as the institution in which he encounters God in Christ. For the Church has the baptism, the Eucharist, the grace of love and the hope of eternal life, and this is everything. We can be truly impatient for reform in accordance with the nature of the Church only if this knowledge remains alive in us. Otherwise we shall have missed the true starting point and our reforms will end in the deformation of what is most essential. Holy impatience is the fruit of patient love which believes all, hopes all, bears all, which is not embittered but forgiving, which can wait and is prepared to sow a seed which others will reap, which gives without being sure in advance that it will also receive.

In this way we all ought to be impatient, everyone according to his place. We ought to belong to those who long for the kingdom of God which is also the end of the earthly Church, and who work for this Church so that she may become a credible sign of the powerful love of

God which reconciles all and brings about his kingdom. The Second Vatican Council has said that Christians should impregnate even the structures of secular life with their eschatological hope; hence this hope must not be misunderstood as dispensing us from being active in the world and reforming it, an attitude which is even more necessary for the Christian's relation to the Church. The Church, too, always remains the responsibility of the Christian; she is not only the permanent institution that mediates his personal salvation. The Church, too, is always what we make her, and we make her what we are ourselves. If we are full of holy impatience, living in faith, hope and love of God and men, if we always hope against hope, then the Church, too, will become what she ought to be. God will certainly always create such men and women. But his grace also gives us the responsibility and the power ourselves to belong to those who do not only want to be supported by the Church, but who themselves help to support her with courage, confidence and patience.

Compulsory Alternatives

In the last two essays we have tried to say something about the post-conciliar situation of the Church, and we had to distinguish between two types of Catholics. There was first the worried Catholic who thought that too much had been changed and everything had become insecure, and secondly the impatient Catholic for whom the programme of the Council was realized too slowly. We should now like to say something that concerns both types of Catholic in the same way, making some general remarks on compulsory alternatives. They should really be quite commonplace, nevertheless we can better understand the situation of the Church and the tensions involved in it if we consider more exactly this principle of compulsory alternatives for both sides.

This principle means first: In ecclesiastical decisions, measures, etc., there is always a choice between at least two, but usually between a number of possibilities. For in the case of the individual as well as of a society, including the Church, there are always many possibilities from which, however, only one can be chosen at a time for common action in so far as this is necessary. Even abstention from a choice, a policy of neutrality and drifting are decisions, but they do not ultimately dispense from the necessity and the torment to choose one from many possibilities. For one could also do something else. There are many possible ecclesiastical languages, many ways of priestly life, many possible methods of the care of souls, various ways of distributing Church moneys, diverse forms of cooperation between laity and clergy, many possible ways of establishing the relations between the Church and society, the state and so forth. If the Church is not to disintegrate, only one of all these possibilities can be realized at a given time. Here, too, the principle applies that one can drive either on the right or on the left but not on both sides at the same time; we must make a choice. Moreover, except in the question of truth, all these possibilities have something in their favour, hence we cannot say that we are choosing the only right thing among the various possibilities, otherwise they would all be wrong.

Nearly every choice is the choice of something meaningful involving the loss of another possibility, which would have had its own special good points which are not present in what has finally been chosen. But all men, including the conservatives as well as the progressives in the Church, are always tempted to recommend the decision of their own choice by proclaiming it to be the only right and sensible one, and by completely denigrating the other alternative. They are afraid of damaging the chance of their own proposal if they admit the slightest good in that of their opponent. However, a free man, and especially a sincere Christian, will know that only God is the infinite good without any negative admixture; he ought therefore to regard his own proposal in a spirit of criticism and to acknowledge the good qualities of that of his opponent. He should also know that one must choose humbly and critically between several possibilities, none of which is absolutely preferable to the other. How different would be the certainly inevitable controversies in the Church if all parties would fight honestly, admitting the weaknesses and dangers of their own position, if they would only acknowledge at least the speck in their own eye while they think themselves obliged to take exception to the log in the eye of their neighbour.

We Christians ought to know that we can only conquer in a Christian spirit if we have ourselves increased the danger of our defeat by honestly admitting the weakness of our own position. A bishop must defend his own authority by also acknowledging his failures; a layman must plead for greater rights for the laity by also regretting the frequent indifference of the laity; we all should not only praise our own plan but also show up its weaknesses. Then we would begin to conduct our own controversies within the Church in a Christian spirit. Otherwise we shall, from the Christian point of view, remain obstinate egoists who fundamentally fight for themselves rather than for their object. If we elevate our own good plan to the only good plan we make an idol of it. But then we should not be Christians but, at best, very clever propagandists. We should train ourselves to develop an instinct to distinguish between those proposals which are to be presented modestly, charitably and critically and others that should be abandoned. This might be useful for the discernment of spirits. The way in which the Pope and his measures are frequently criticized today betray a presumption which is itself hardly Christian.

What has been said about the necessity of alternatives must still be clarified. For if an alternative in ecclesiastical matters is truly good, it is so because it accords with the permanent principles of Christianity. However, even so it cannot be said to be the only correct line. Now this is the real crux of these necessary alternatives. For whoever advocates a certain course of action must base his recommendation on Christian principles and try to show that it corresponds to them. This is both his right and his duty. At the same time he must usually not behave as if his idea were the only legitimate way of realizing Christian principles, because this is not normally the case, the opposite view being also a genuine Christian possibility. And it is indeed difficult to do only the one and abandon the other. For there is, on the one hand, a connection between these Christian principles and a proposed programme while, on the other, this connection is not compelling. This shows that a choice between these various possibilities needs decisions, and these cannot be arrived at by theoretical considerations alone. For not only is theory never effective in real life, but even at best theoretical reason by itself cannot make a practical decision.

For example, it cannot be decided by any theological reflection alone whether or not the tabernacle is best placed on the main altar. There are reasons for as well as against. In this case the decision does not depend only on theological considerations. *That* something is wanted is an addition to the reasons *why* it is wanted. Hence in the case of theological decisions there will not only be a conflict of theoretical reasons but also a struggle of wills. This is not a bad thing, for it belongs to the nature of human existence. But we must know this and not pretend in theoretical disputes that it is otherwise. Else the discussion would be poisoned, because it would have to be supposed that the opponent is stupid or narrow-minded; and in this case we could no longer realize that such disputes also have a moral element, namely love, respect for the other's attitude and tolerance.

Such virtues are a possible element of true controversy, because this can never be determined by the theoretical reason alone. Thus it also becomes clear that not every compromise is necessarily a betrayal of reason and one's own better judgment: it may be the choice of an alternative that has good reasons in its favour, but beside which there are other possibilities which are not bad either. To choose thus is not undignified. There will always be enough obstinate people who can prevent the wisdom of such relativism from deteriorating into indifference. But if we realize the relativity of a certain decision we cannot rightly pretend that we advocate something absolute.

In my view much could be improved in the inevitable struggles between conservatives and progressives in the Church if the nature of this necessity of alternatives were better understood. This does not mean that controversies are to be avoided. On the contrary, they are inevitable because decisions in the sense described above cannot be made otherwise. Nor will all alternatives be equally good, and therefore it will have to be discussed which is better in a certain case. Nevertheless, a deeper consideration of "compulsory alternatives" would show what is at the bottom of it, namely the course of history which cannot be guided by theoretical reason alone, but demands decisions which might also have been different and must be accepted by all in the unity of the Church, despite their admitted contingency. Both conservatives and progressives ought to understand that the reality which is lived in the Church in love and humility is better than a possibility for which both parties rightly fight, so that one thing may become reality which will then be the truly Christian thing for both.

Present Tasks

The following suggestions may perhaps become important for the immediate future of the Church if Christianity endeavours to do justice to the situation in which it must accomplish its mission. Of course, these proposals are not a catalogue of absolute norms nor a panacea for the Church of today, for they will always remain problematic by their very nature. They cease to be interesting and practically fruitful if they are concerned with absolutely everything and recommend all that is useful and desirable. But they become problematical if they make a choice and stress certain points which are necessary for finite human action, because this cannot realize everything at once and can be successful only in contingency. For who is to say what is most necessary here and now? Even if such proposals are made by competent authority they can be only tentative impulses, while the ultimate actual line of development cannot be defined by any human authority but must be left solely to the Lord of history.

For the future of the Church everywhere, too, what is most essential is the ancient yet ever-new message of Christianity, that is to say that in the darkness of this life the hearts of men must entrust themselves to that ineffable, adorable mystery of life which we call God in faith, hope and love and unconditional confidence in Jesus Christ our

Lord. Apart from this everything else the Church can do in her official activity is but the mediation of salvation which is, indeed, absolutely necessary, but which must nevertheless be distinguished from that on which ultimately everything depends, as has been said before, namely on the faith, hope and love in the hearts of men. We must, indeed, consider how the Church should act in the present as well as in the future, we must organize and interest ourselves in her social side; but all this must always serve only these ancient and ever-new truths. There is the danger that owing to the will to reform initiated by the Council Catholics are no longer sufficiently aware of this simple truth. Today, too, what is most important is prayer, love of Jesus Christ, silence and suffering, indeed all the things that the good old tradition of the Church has always known and lived. We shall certainly have to take great pains to announce this ancient message in new forms so that it may enter the hearts and minds of modern men. Certainly its eternal validity must not be abused to defend a boring traditionalism that has gone stale. But just those who have welcomed the Council and its almost revolutionary *aggiornamento* and are fired with a radical reforming zeal must ask themselves whether they really want to serve the true spirit of Christianity and to confess the folly of the cross. True, we must adapt ourselves to the contemporary situation, and this has often been omitted by a traditionalist obstinacy and a pusillanimous desire for self-preservation; but if we adapt ourselves to our time this must only be for the purpose of converting our fellow men from their idols so that they may serve the true and living God and await the return of Jesus, his Son, whom he has raised from the dead and who will save us from the wrath to come (1 Thess 1:9f.). All liturgical renewal, all changes in the education and way of life of priests, all

adaptation of the religious orders to contemporary conditions, the activities of mature laymen as well as the frank
dialogue with the present world, all these must only serve
the love of God and one's neighbour in the unfeigned faith
which will always be foolishness and scandal to the wise
and prudent of this world. All reformers even of fossilized
traditions, however legitimate their desires, must realize
that they will have to give an account before God and not
only before their contemporaries, and that it is not *a priori*
evident that both judgments will agree.

If we are bold enough to say something about the last
strategical and tactical principles of the Church in the
Western world as we envisage them for the next few
decades, we are nevertheless well aware that God directs
history, while man makes plans which will certainly not
be realized in the way they were conceived. But this does
not dispense us from making plans, and even in ecclesial
matters it does not permit us to live from day to day,
wanting to hold God responsible for what man has to do.
This is true especially in a period of history in which man
has been burdened with deciding his own destiny in far
greater measure than it has ever been the case, and even
possible, before.

Today such fundamental principles of ecclesiastical
strategy and tactics can no longer, as in the age of paternalism, be left only to the Church authorities, who, in their
wisdom, would make their decisions, guided simply by
their own instinct and the assistance of the Holy Spirit.
The ecclesiastical authorities have certainly the last word
and are entitled to expect willing obedience. But today
this does not exclude but rather implies that such questions
are publicly discussed in the Church and that the faithful
take part in considering and advising on them. Of course,
such discussions must be carried on with tact and discretion

and will rightly and inevitably be guided by the ecclesiastical authorities. But today we need no longer fear that
they will do much harm and make the laity less willing
to abide by the decisions of the hierarchy. Secret diplomacy
is no longer profitable. In the end it will harm confidence
and willing obedience more than the public discussion even
of delicate questions, because they are well known in any
case and can be discussed more objectively in public than
if they are only debated in small fanatical circles. Even
today Catholics are not dispensed of obedience, but have
to learn that they must willingly also do things that are
not obvious to them if they have been decided on by the
authorities of the Church.

The Church of Personal Faith

There are norms of ecclesial action which are valid for all
times, because they derive from the very nature of Christianity, and they, of course, remain the most important.
But apart from these there is also the fact that the Church
in much of the traditionally Christian world is still on the
way from being an established Church (that is, a social
institution to which all more or less belong) to a Church
of personal faith in a pluralistic society. We ought not to
make absolute or glorify either the *terminus a quo* or the
terminus ad quem of this movement. In other words,
neither must the former social position of the Church be
defended as far as possible in all circumstances, nor must
her future social position which is still only partly present
be regarded as absolutely desirable. We must first simply
consider facts, from which certain principles of action
may be derived even before the foreseeable development
is either condemned or praised. The future Church in

central Europe will enjoy less legal and institutional power than before. If neither her past nor her future are to be considered as absolutely desirable, two opposing principles are ruled out. For we shall neither defend her former social position as far as at all possible, nor shall we want to make her give up whatever is still left of this historical position as fast as possible and of her own free will. It may well be that one does not want to give up voluntarily what one still possesses, though one has to reckon with the possibility of losing it; it may also be that it is better to give up something voluntarily so as to be better prepared for the future when one will not possess it in any case. There are both conservative and progressive "simplifiers" who would decide the question what is best to be done here and now by eternal principles instead of by prudent practical considerations. If one does the latter, it is of course clear that even a correct or at least meaningful possible decision will not appear as indisputably necessary, and thus a man will not be absolved of his duty to decide into uncertainty. With these reservations we might well be of the opinion that the Church in Germany, and not only there, is, on the whole, still tempted to defend old conservative positions rather than to surrender them in order to prepare even now for an inevitable future, despite some conciliar courage to start anew and risk an uncertain future. The courage to "mobile warfare" does seem to be less than would be desirable. For where in present-day German Catholicism are there really bold experiments?

Concentrating Ecclesiastical Action

It is further necessary for the strategy of the Church that the authorities should have the courage to concentrate their attention on certain definite points. The Church, too, cannot do all that might be good and useful at the same time. She should certainly not become onesided, expecting everything from a gimmick, but she must not want to do everything with the same energy either; she must have the courage to concentrate her finite powers on a few points, even though this will mean giving up other important things. If we take this into consideration as well as the position of the Church in a pluralistic society, we shall realize that today the Church cannot want to care directly for all groups and individuals of our society in equal measure. For this we are simply not strong enough, we would only waste our efforts if we wanted to influence society directly in the way of the former "people's Church". In an increasingly scientific and technological society governed by experts, the Church ought not primarily to address the "people", which in any case will soon cease to exist, but rather the "educated classes". This should be done not, indeed, because these might be worthier of eternal life or even easier to influence, but because the salvation of all will depend on the acceptance of Christianity by the leaders of society.

Courage and Self-Confidence of the Preachers of the Gospel

Courage and self-confidence of the bearers of the Christian message should be a third fundamental principle of the strategy of the Church. Precisely in view of the Church's situation the preachers of the gospel ought not to think themselves condemned to being always on the defensive. We easily regard as the defeat and regression of the Church in modern times what is actually only the social mani-

festation of a state which has always existed, even in the
so-called good old days, because even then people, on the
average, had but little faith, hope and love of God and
men. Only formerly this was not so obvious, because
society was homogeneous, not, indeed, because of the power
of grace and the Church, but simply for secular reasons.
On the other hand, even from a purely natural point of
view Christianity, properly preached and lived, is still a
match for every other powerful propagandist *Weltanschauung*, though men's hardness of heart is often an
obstacle to its acceptance.

How the Suggestions of the Council are to be Realized

After these very general remarks I should now like to
make some more positive suggestions. First of all, we
should try as hard as we can to carry out both the spirit
and the letter of the Council. Because the German bishops
belonged to the progressive party of the Council we ought
not to imagine that there is nothing left for us to do. The
Constitution on the Liturgy confronts us with many tasks
which are still outstanding, especially as the Bishops' Conferences have been given considerable competences in this
field which should be used courageously. Will the bishops
have the courage to use the possibilities provided by the
Constitution on the Church with regard to the renewal of
the diaconate? Will the German Bishops' Conference give
itself a statute that really makes it a collegial institution
capable of effective action? The Decree on the Bishops has
confronted the German Church, too, with the question of
the correct size and definition of the dioceses. It cannot be
said that the principles according to which this question
must be answered are sufficiently clear and that there is the

determination to act on these principles even if local interests may sometimes get hurt in the process.

The Council has entrusted the Bishops' Conference with working out a new order for the education and training of priests in accordance with contemporary and local needs. Here much will have to be considered and courageously changed. It would be desirable that seminaries and theological faculties should lay less stress on apologetics and the defense of existing conditions. They should put into practice a new conception of theological education which would serve first and foremost the preaching of the gospel, and only secondarily the interests of scholarship for its own sake. They should also lay great emphasis on the living unity of priestly existence and spiritual life so as to overcome the doubts and difficulties of our theological students as well as of the science of theology itself. In this connection it should, of course, also be considered how the seminary life of the future priests could be changed so that it would not unwittingly militate against the intellectually and religiously stronger human personalities.

At the Council ecumenism has certainly gained a greater victory than could possibly have been hoped for even twenty years ago. But this should not obscure the fact that almost everything has still to be done where the unity of divided Christendom is concerned. Real successes in this sphere cannot be forced or achieved prematurely. Nor do concrete results depend only on the good will of the Catholic partner. Sometimes one even has the impression that Protestant authorities will, indeed, ask what Catholics are prepared to do, but are less inclined to say how far they themselves will meet the Catholic side. But we shall have to admit that Catholics, too, are reluctant to take the first step before knowing how the others are going to react. In the present situation of Christendom the Churches ought to do everything to promote their unity except what their faith actually forbids; but this principle of true ecumenical action is as yet by no means recognized and obeyed.

The Council admonishes the bishops to realize their responsibility for the whole Church. It is to be hoped that this responsibility will produce greater results than the financing of charitable schemes such as *Misereor* and *Adveniat*. Despite the shortage of priests the Church in central and western Europe ought to have the courage, and the clergy the generosity, to put secular priests at the disposal of the missions and of Latin America.

Within the next decade we shall have assiduously to canvass the question whether the religious orders and congregations will really put into practice the Decree on the Appropriate Renewal of the Religious Life, whether they will produce a style of life and of government which, on the one hand, is truly suitable for our time and, on the other, is seriously engaged only in the service of Christ.

The Decree on the Missions sets all European Churches the task of conquering a missionary defeatism due to the idea that the end of the age of colonialism and imperialism also spells the end of the missionary age.

In the Constitution on the Church there is much that has so far remained only on paper. For we are still very far from experiencing the Church of Christ as the highest realization of the presence of Christ and the unity of love in the local eucharistic community.

The Decree on the Ministry and Life of Priests is perhaps still too much determined by an ideal which originated in the social order of the past. But this makes it all the more important to develop a pattern which corresponds to the social and intellectual situation of the present and the future. This must not, however, betray the true vocation of the priest, who is not simply entrusted with conducting a few services every week, but has the frightening duty to proclaim the word of God and to bring the message of Christ to the particular situation of the individual whether it is acceptable or not, and who, in the sacrifice of the community, announces the death of the Lord till he comes again. Even the Council is aware that this may sometimes happen in combination with a secular profession.

The dialogue with the contemporary world enjoined on the Church in the Pastoral Constitution on the Church in the Modern World is still in its infancy. For there is a wide-spread tradition which tries to keep the Church in a self-sufficient isolation instead of risking herself in the service of the world and of all men.

From a general as well as from the pastoral point of view it would be wrong to assume that the Church in the various countries needed only to follow the directives of the Council willingly and exactly in order to fulfill her God-given task in this time. Certainly, the Council has given our contemporary theologians the task to explain and justify its doctrine, which will occupy them for a long time. But if they were concerned chiefly with conciliar ecclesiology or with commenting on the Constitution on Divine Revelation they would by-pass the main duty laid upon them today.

This is quite obvious if we have really understood the true intention of the Pastoral Constitution on the Church in the Modern World. For the dialogue with contemporary life which has been imposed on the Church cannot refer to what she and her members can contribute to improve social conditions in the world. Her one great inescapable duty it to proclaim the living God and his forgiving and deifying nearness in his grace through Jesus Christ. In view of the religious distress of contemporary men theologians must once more consider the central themes of

Christian preaching, which are God, the incarnation of the eternal Word in Jesus Christ, grace and eternal life. They cannot assume that everything about these subjects is quite clear and that all that needs to be done is for the preacher to proclaim the theology of the schools as best he can from the pulpit. Theological science itself has not yet tackled even in theory the phenomenon of a worldwide atheism that appears self-evident to itself. We do not yet possess a mystagogy in the experience of God and his grace which would be practicable for the ordinary pastor and which would appeal to our sceptical, scientifically trained contemporaries. We need much thought and practice before we can preach the mystery of the incarnation of the eternal Logos in Jesus of Nazareth in such a way that this message does not sound almost like a myth in which modern men can no longer believe. The theology of salvation history is still far from being worked out sufficiently to be easily credible to a person who knows that human history is perhaps a million years old and that the large mayority of men have not been reached by the message of the gospel. In order to do justice to the spirit and intention of the Council theologians must do more than merely consider the letter of its doctrinal declarations.

Educating Mature Christians

Though the Council has brought and will still bring many blessings, it has certainly also produced dangers for the Church and her life. This is true even if we should perhaps rather say more cautiously that these dangers have become manifest through the Council, and that all this is a crisis of growth. But even a crisis of growth is a crisis and has its dangers. The danger is this, to put it bluntly, that many Christians are tempted to believe no longer in the infallibility of the Church's doctrine and to make light of its directives for the life and practice of the individual as well as of the Church.

a. Unchangeable Principles and Changeable Directives

The reasons for this danger are, of course, psychological rather than actually theoretical. According to the traditional teaching of the Church truly educated theologians have always distinguished between irreformable definitions of the magisterium and authoritative, but actually reformable doctrinal utterances of the Church. Beyond this, there are the more or less unanimous opinions of theologians. Theologians can also understand that a teaching of the Church is not a *quantité négligeable*, even if it is not proposed as an absolutely binding and irreformable doctrine of the divine and Catholic faith. According to quite traditional teaching they can distinguish also between principles of action that are of divine and immutable law, and positive ecclesiastical decrees which are changeable.

Hence the Council cannot reasonably be a danger to the theologian. The case of a not theologically trained Christian is different, for he is usually unaware of these distinctions. Nor are they easily intelligible, especially as regards their application. We should also admit in all honesty that in the general practice of the Church these distinctions are suppressed rather than clarified as far as the faithful are concerned. In the past the Church has appeared to many Catholics as an absolutely monolithic structure, a system of doctrine and life which had to be either accepted or rejected as a whole, without degrees or nuances of importance in its various components. And many considered this view, which is certainly not that of the Church herself, as the actual characteristic of Catholicism, which was proudly acclaimed as the opposite of liberalistic contradictions.

b. A Right Understanding of the Teaching Office

Further, the ordinary Christian unversed in church history could hardly experience changes in Catholic doctrine and life, because his own life was too short and ecclesial development too slow. Hence he can, for example, be of the opinion that the Church could give up the indissolubility of sacramental marriage just as well as the ecclesial form of contracting a marriage, or that she could change the very principles of sexual morality because formerly she took a different authoritative, though not definitive, view of their application, which will perhaps have to be revised.

Moreover, people often do not know how the magisterium arrives, indeed must arrive, at an ultimately binding decision. The popular idea leaves out the necessary human element of study, of the consultation of experts and theologians, of discussion with its inevitable clash of opinions. The Church has always recognized this human element, but the general idea is that the highest authority must decide at once, almost like a *deus ex machina,* if the decision is to be considered really binding. It is wrongly assumed that if the Pope is not to compromise his authority he ought to decide every dogmatic or moral question that comes up, preferably at once. In fact, however, Paul V for example never decided the controversy on grace which greatly exercised the minds at the time and which was endlessly debated by theological commissions in Rome. It is still open today and will almost certainly not be decided in the future either.

In this situation the Church has a new and very difficult duty of educating people, which will certainly take a long time. The sometimes almost desperate conservatives must be taught to understand, not only theoretically but instinctively and in their spiritual life, that the Church does not exist outside time and history; that she is indeed founded on the grace of Christ, but is nevertheless a very human institution burdened by history. They must realize that her understanding of the faith and the practice of her life must be courageously changed, if she is to remain the pillar of truth and the home of Christian existence. The wildly revolutionary Christians, on the other hand, must be patiently taught that also today and in the future the Church is an authoritatively teaching "absolute system", and that we can modestly yet frankly make only those objections to it which she formally recognizes as belonging to this system, even though nothing is said about their contents.

c. Responsibility in Free Obedience

This is the real task when we attempt to form the much discussed Christian-come-of-age. He must learn more than ever before to bear his own responsibility within the concrete Church and not in a basic, though secret opposition to her, and to cope also with the historical conditions of her doctrine and practice in freely given obedience. He must learn to understand that, if he is not to prefer his own self-will to the will of Christ, his conscience needs the authoritative decisions and directives of the Church, even if these do not involve her supreme authority. Of course, if such principles are to influence human life they need a certain casuistry which we cannot develop here, but which is necessary and which both priests and laity must be able to apply. There is even quite frequently a certain difference between what can be justified before the forum of the Church and what is allowed or even demanded by conscience. This is a difference that cannot be dissolved in every case, hence the individual Christian must learn to bear it with patience and courage without letting it degenerate into a fundamental opposition to the Church. The education of the Christian who has come of age in this sense is perhaps much more important than many other tasks that are emphasized today. It must begin with the clergy. For priests, too, are not necessarily immune against misunderstanding the historicity of the Church's doctrine and practice either from an irritable conservatism or from revolutionary progressivism.

Individual Morality Rightly Understood

Difference between Theoretical and Real Morality

It is clear from all this that it will be one of the great duties of the Church to take perhaps more account than before of the moral questions confronting the Christian in his daily life and to approach them frankly and courageously. For given not only the sinfulness but also the limitations of human beings, there will always be a difference between the official morality proclaimed by the Church and that which is practised by the average Christian. True, the Church cannot adapt the moral demands of the gospel to the statistics of average morality. It is certainly not *a priori* impossible that the Church might be led into almost insoluble and humanly hopeless difficulties, not only as regards the morality of certain individuals, but also the public morals of society or large groups. In such a situation the Church may finally have no other choice than to remain faithful to the gospel and to proclaim the hard message of the holy God, leaving everything else to the grace of him who can certainly also save men in a situation in which the Church can do no more.

But this fundamentally certainly correct principle, too, must be applied with caution. If in relatively normal circumstances there is too great a gap between the theoretical morality of the Church and what is actually practised even by good Catholics, the Church will have to ask herself whether she has really done all that was necessary as far as the working out of her doctrine in pastoral practice is concerned. The latest theological development in the question of birth control, for example, surely shows that moral theology has not yet done everything possible so as not to let the gap become too wide. This example shows that one fundamental question has not yet been sufficiently considered theoretically, let alone practically solved. This question concerns what the Church should do or not do if society or groups are in a state which, on the individual plane, would be considered as invincible and inculpable error.

In the case of the individual living *bona fide* in invincible error, moral theologians have worked out useful principles which make life easier regarding the practice of the confessional, admission to the sacraments and so forth. But it can hardly be doubted that such a state of actually invincible error in moral questions exists also in society or in social groups in which the individual participates, so that his power of moral discernment does not go beyond a certain point, which, through no fault of his own, falls below objective morality.

Objective and Subjective Guilt

There need not be truly subjective guilt either in the case of the individual or of a social group, even when the subjective conscience is confronted with the official teaching of the Church as a formally binding authority. For in such a case, too, the moral judgment (that is the capacity of subjective realization) may remain below objective demand even despite normal intelligence and freedom, and though the objective demand has been understood and the fundamental authority of the Church is not disputed. What is the Church to do in such a case, so that, on the one hand, she will do justice to an irremediable situation and, on the other, not betray her vocation to announce the gospel in its integrity and thus slowly to change this situation? The Church will not, for example, be able to baptize an African chieftain who wants to keep his harem; yet she may, in certain circumstances, judge that he has a subjectively good conscience (though he has heard the message of the gospel and is willing in principle to believe in it), because in his actual social and human circumstances he cannot yet realize the moral demand of monogamy, as little as formerly king David and king Solomon. But if the Church cannot actually baptize such a chieftain, there are still questions waiting for an answer, for example, how she is to behave towards him, and how as positive a relationship as possible can be achieved on both sides.

The Problem of Divorce

Theoretically, too, the question has not yet been answered what the Church is to do in the case of an insurmountable difference between theoretical and practical morality. Even less are both clergy and laity accustomed to solve it in practice. This is presumably not only the case with regard to birth control, but also with regard to the second urgent pastoral problem, namely divorce. The Church can certainly not give up the principle of the indissolubility of a consummated sacramental marriage, because she is bound by the words of Christ in the gospel, even, despite a single contrary intervention at the Council, in the case of an innocent party. Nevertheless, one relevant question has not been clarified nearly enough. It is this: what personal conditions must be present in the contemporary human and social situation to guarantee in a concrete case that will to marriage which alone constitutes an insoluble union? Does it really suffice that the partners should have a superficial knowledge of the substance of marriage, be of average intelligence and without *vis et metus*, as matrimonial canon law requires? Moreover, there is another question that has not been sufficiently cleared up in theory, and for which no practical solution has been found. What should be done by the Church and the individual Christian if a marriage has broken down and there is an insuperable difference between the decision of a subjectively and objectively good and right conscience and that of the Church? No one can seriously maintain that contemporary conditions are not such that these cases become much more numerous, a situation that cannot be prevented by legal measures.

Necessary Conditions and Dangers of a "Morality of Conscience"

Thus we have approached a whole complex of tasks and questions which the Church and her pastors will have to tackle more frankly and courageously in the near future. The Church will certainly not fall for the wrong and over-simple solution of a situation ethics. But even without such a heretical solution she will realize that in view of the complicated conditions of our time in the moral sphere, too, many cases can no longer be decided directly by the official judgment of the Church, but must be left to the individual conscience guided by the great norms of the gospel which she announces. Now some people might object to such a rightly understood individual morality, saying that it allows Christians to act in an arbitrary manner with the result that they will drift into a moral laxism, always taking the easier line even if it does not all correspond to the spirit of the gospel. But such an objection would only prove that Christians have frequently been wrongly educated, that they have unintentionally been imbued with the idea that they are allowed to do anything not explicitly forbidden by the authorities of the Church and that one has less confidence in the power of the gospel and its grace than in detailed external moral prescriptions. There can be no doubt that many Christians are of the opinion that whatever is not apodictically forbidden from the pulpit is permissible. But the Church must overcome this mentality by patient teaching. This duty cannot be replaced by ever more subtle casuistry intended to regulate everything to the minutest detail. This task, too, is more urgent than many others which are only too often regarded as of paramount importance.

The Future Relationship between the "Estates of the Church"

Clergy and Laity

The transition of an established Church to a Church of the community of faith already poses very pressing problems.

These exist even if one does not believe that we ought to accelerate this slow transition to an almost suicidal surrender of legitimate historical positions which are profitable for salvation and which the Church still occupies in present-day society. As has already been stressed, here the conservatives as well as the revolutionaries start from presuppositions which are objectively quite unjustified, for they regard either the past or the future of the Church as an ideal state. But even if neither is accepted, we suggest that there are certain things which the Church ought not only resignedly to await but which she might well go forward to meet. As has been said before, it is to be expected that in future the type of the Church both in the diocese and in the parish will be that of a community of faith in a pluralistic society. Hence she will scarcely still occupy social positions which are independent of the truly personal religious convictions of her members, for she will no longer be a people's church to which men belong without such a personal decision. Now if this is the case, then the relation between clergy and laity in such a community Church of faith will differ considerably from what it still is inevitably today.

Clergy and laity will then experience themselves first of all as brothers of the same religious mind and conviction which all have acquired through many sacrifices in a personal decision and in conscious opposition to the mentality of their surroundings. There will then no longer be a "power struggle" between both groups, or if it still exists it will take quite a harmless form, as is the case also in other informal groups which are united to each other for better or worse. In such a community Church the laity will, of course, respect the special vocation of the clergy, but the latter will no longer appear to them as a social group whose religious mission involves real power which is not dependent on the faith and good will of the laity. In such a situation the Church will be able to concede to the laity as much power as is possible within her divine constitution, without thereby endangering the special mission and the specifically religious authority of the clergy. Conversely, the laity will no longer feel themselves treated as minors by the clergy because the priests, too, will be seen to be guided in their task by the same personally acquired convictions as everyone else. The Church might well already begin to meet this situation. At the Council it has often rightly been said that the laity are not only objects of the Church's saving activities but are subjects together with the clergy, that they have their own mission and responsibility in and for the Church, and that they may, indeed in certain circumstances must, also take part in activities which are the more immediate concern of the clergy. But in view of these declarations of the Council it has to be stressed that such active cooperation in tasks which belong primarily to the clergy can be satisfactorily achieved only if it is furnished also with corresponding rights, which must be established by law and not left to the good pleasure of individual bishops and parish priests. Such legal fixation of the tasks and corresponding rights of the laity could already be undertaken, so that the directives and ideals of the Council may not remain merely on paper. We need not perhaps introduce the election of parish priests by the laity such as has been and still is the custom in the Catholic cantons of Switzerland, without the divine constitution of the Church being thereby endangered. But there are surely many possibilities to make it clear also by legislation that laymen have not only the right to receive the sacraments from the clergy, as the present Code of Canon Law states. If the future Church is to have laymen who cooperate responsibly in the tasks of the Church, then surely it is time to begin to train them and to give them a share in the decisions of the Church, even if the administration would function more smoothly without them.

The Problem of the Shortage of Priests

It is perhaps right to consider the problem of the shortage of priests from the same point of view. For this shortage would seem to be by no means so acute if the Church were to entrust the laity with whatever is not prohibited to them by the divine and immutable law of her constitution. To do this would be quite possible, seeing that our laity are very educated and have a considerable amount of spare time. Add to this that the possibilities of the permanent diaconate of married men of mature age have not been at all exhausted. It may therefore be asked how great is the shortage of priests, if we would gradually make the change to a community church of faith.

For if this were done there is another question which places the problem of the shortage of priests under another aspect, which has been discussed before. Up to now the distribution of the clergy has been made according to the principle that every baptized Catholic would have to be looked after directly by a priest. If this principle is applied also to those who do not practise their faith, hence have no real relation to the community Church of faith, then the actual number of priests must, indeed, give the impression of a shortage, for there are not even enough priests for all the established parishes and Mass centres. This conception has inevitably the further consequence that, apart from the priests in the ecclesiastical administration and a few others, all the clergy must be deployed in the parishes. Hence there are hardly any available to care for free, "charismatic", formal or informal groups which are not organized according to the territorial principle. This is aggravated by the tendency, due to various reasons including financial ones, to employ even the regular clergy in the ordinary care of souls. This lack of an as it were "mobile" clergy may well be damaging for the living presence of the Church in a pluralist society, for such a clergy might be aware of new tasks, and make use of special gifts and contacts due to their former professional and general experience. The harm done by the absence of such "free-lance" priests might even be greater in the long run than the momentary inability to reach all Catholics as equally and directly as possible. This is not meant to belittle the dignity and importance of the "ordinary care of souls" with its unselfish service and its daily burden. But in a pluralist society of general education and at a time when the community Church of faith is bound to come, we should surely consider whether the spiritual tactics of the people's Church are still viable, and if the "shortage of priests" does not partly stem from this.

In a future community Church of faith there might also be sacramentally ordained "elders" (Greek *presbyteroi* — priests) who need not necessarily have passed through all the stages of the modern education and training of priests, an education which was at least partly determined by the fact that the clergy were a sociological "class" among others. This is another consideration which might help to overcome the shortage of priests; for there might well be priests who would be suitable for such a Church of faith and have authority, even though they would be received into the clergy as mature men after a quite differently conceived training.

A few years ago an Austrian Catholic lay congress met under the motto: Do not extinguish the Spirit. Despite the

Council we should today perhaps have to say: Arouse the Spirit. True, he is always a gift of God, who governs the Church without having to give an account to us. The Council has also warned against expecting special, arresting charisms in the Church. Nevertheless, we are bound to hope and pray that God may give to his Church the power of a courageous spirit which risks the future, even though this spirit should also include special and unexpected charismatic gifts. Whe should not only not extinguish such a spirit, but should try rather to arouse it. The Council has shown that such a spirit that dares what is new is still alive in the Church. Its utterances will necessarily either be in danger of being contradicted by obstinate "old believers" (such as happened also in Montanism, Novatianism, Donatism down reactionary Jansenism and Integralism) or of being falsified by a mentality which betrays the spirit of Christ, the folly of the cross and the courage to contradict a world lying in the Evil One by cheap "adaptation". The Church, trusting in her Spirit, must find her way between these two dangers.

II. CHRISTIAN FAITH —
THE DELIVERANCE OF THE WORLD

Faith and Culture

Today faith and religion are often judged by their usefulness. Our contemporaries demand instinctively that faith should prove its value in the world of our experience, it should produce a better world, foster peace, mitigate or abolish social tensions and generally make life more bearable. Otherwise, it is thought, it need not exist at all. In view of this naive prejudice we would first ask quite simply: why must faith do all this in order to be acceptable? Is not man precisely the being that also has other aims? Does he not want truth, even if it causes suffering, beauty, even though it is useless, the holy in order to adore it? Does he not find the right relation to consumer goods and luxuries just when he is detached from them because he is aware of another sphere and selflessly worships that which is of no direct "use" to him?

We had to make this brief reservation before discussing "faith and culture". For though the sphere of culture itself belongs partly to the realm of truth, beauty and holiness which ultimately has no need to defend itself before the court of utilitarianism, faith and its object transcend even these good things. For they are concerned with God and his salvation, which men can receive only if they adore him who is the first and last mystery of their existence in selfless hope and love.

Keeping in mind this reservation, we may now, however, discuss a positive mutual relationship between faith
and culture. Without quoting too extensively we here follow particularly section two of the second chapter of the
Pastoral Constitution of Vatican II on the Church in the
Modern World. For this chapter deals precisely with this
subject, namely the proper development of culture and
the importance of the Christian faith for this development.

We cannot here answer the question of what culture is.
We can only just mention the cultural inheritance received
by the individual such as scholarship, art in all its forms,
morality and religion, which transcends morality and
which despite its superior nature is also a cultural phenomenon, determining and being determined by the culture
of a nation and an epoch. Culture may be defined as an
element of tradition which helps to determine a man's
surroundings and which man himself not only receives
and accepts, but also develops through his free creative
work as something that is specifically human. Such cultural
work is not a luxury in which a man indulges, because
without it a man could not even exist as a natural being.
In this context we should like to warn against the snobbery
of certain circles who imagine that natural science, technology and social planning have nothing to do with culture, which in their view can only be created by individualistic élites. We would add to this that one must distinguish between culture such as it is and as it ought to be.
For culture can be judged by critical standards: indeed,
such a critical attitude which demands change is an essential element of culture itself. Further, the ideal culture,
too, is no timeless entity but has itself a history in time
and space, so that many ideals of culture exist beside the
actual cultures. Hence we are justified in restricting our
subject to the question what the Christian faith could and

should achieve for a contemporary culture such as it ought
to be.

Faith demands responsibility before God also for the
culture which is and remains secular. At first sight this
statement seems to be valid for all time. But we should
remember that a specifically secular culture exists only
today, and that Christianity does not claim to design this
culture directly according to the principles of the faith,
let alone of the teaching office of the Church. Hence there
is the acute danger that the believer will no longer consider
this secular culture as his religious responsibility before
God, but will regard it as something that interests him as
a human being, but no longer affects him as a Christian.
The Council, too, recognizes the danger (*op. cit.* 43 ff.)
that Christians are only seeking "heavenly things" and
think that earthly matters do not concern them and have
no bearing on their salvation, because these things have
become exclusively secular and human. But the Council
says: "The Christian who neglects his temporal duties
neglects his duties toward his neighbour and even God,
and jeopardizes his eternal salvation." Now the words
about the temporal duties should be read within the context of the Council statements about the relative autonomy
of the secular culture (art. 59), for only thus will the
sentence just quoted receive its full weight. For precisely
that culture which cannot be materially given by faith
and the Church is nevertheless the earthly duty that
determines our eternal salvation. In lonely responsibility
the Christian is confronted with these secular cultural
activities, and these, though not only these, are his Christian vocation and mission.

Unified mass culture is a Christian concern. The Council
document does not regard culture as the preserve of a small
élite of individuals or nations who would have a monopoly

on its development. It speaks quite simply of a "mass culture"; it favours the cultural development of all men and nations. True, it desires that most legitimate civilizations should be preserved, yet it approves of the development of "a more universal form of human culture . . . one which will promote and express the unity of the human race" (art. 54) and favours a powerful international organization which, despite the United Nations, does not yet exist (art. 84). The Council wants both sexes to cooperate responsibly in this culture, and men and women of all social classes as well as all nations, whether rich or poor, to have as active a share in it as possible through education, means of communication, tourism and so forth. The Council fathers knew, of course, that there would always be differences of social status, talent and national character, but in their view great genuine culture does not presuppose the existence of a large number of men who are poor, socially weak and exploited. For them culture is not aristocratic and they do not favour the existence of those who, themselves without culture, make possible the culture of others. This almost socialist (to use an inexact term) characteristic of the Council's idea of culture is certainly in a sense contemporary, because in former times such a programme could not have been realized. Nevertheless, in the last analysis this tendency is determined by the Christian view of man as a creature and child of God destined for eternity. For precisely this reason every human being has the right, in principle, to share in the economic and cultural possessions of mankind. In the opinion of the Council the poor have been promised the kingdom of heaven not in order that others, whether individuals or nations, should alone be and remain rich. Mass culture is not ultimately a goal to be welcomed with enthusiasm. It is fundamentally a very sober programme lacking the charm of many contrasts, indeed it may be regarded as "levelling down". But such a programme is a demand of contemporary Christianity, while we are not going to prejudge the sociological justification of the mostly perjorative term "mass". The Christian faith decisively helps the individual to overcome the difficulties of the cultural situation of our time. The Council document says quite freely that it is impossible to guarantee food and peaceful existence to the immense and fast-growing population of our globe without more socialization, powerful international organizations and public intervention in the economies of individual states as well as of mankind as a whole. This greater socialization is not necessarily a good thing in itself, it is simply a necessity. It certainly involves also, though not only, new ties, very real dangers of men's manipulation by others, new restrictions, growing technologically planned uniformity, an ever-increasing fragmentation of man's work. All this is not necessarily compensated by greater freedom; but it is inevitably part of the guilt, which man ought not to have incurred, but which is now part of his life. Thus the so-called progress will also ever increase or at least alter the burden of existence. Faith can help to bear the burden which the contemporary mass culture imposes on us. This does not mean that faith could be manipulated into becoming such a help. But if we unreservedly believe in God, accepting our responsibility to him and hoping in eternal life, this faith will also help us to bear the narrowness and boredom of our life, which has today become worse rather than better. This faith helps us to carry on, without despairing and trying to make up for the greyness of our present world by escaping into the idolatry of superficial pleasures. Sobriety and resigned acceptance of the inevitable are certainly virtues of contemporary man and his humanism. But they either do not suffice without being founded on faith, or they are already filled unconsciously with what the Christian calls faith.

According to the Council Christians have the duty to impregnate the structures of secular life with their eschatological hope (Dogmatic Constitution on the Church, art. 35, and the Pastoral Constitution on the Church in the Modern World, art. 38). This is an important statement about culture and the Christian's relation to it, for this "secular life" is actually identical with what we call culture. Now this certainly does not mean that the Christians could cause and help to establish their eschatological hope, which is the kingdom of God and ultimately God himself, by their cultural activities. The fulfilment of this hope which God himself freely gives to human history is his own deed and grace. Yet, though the absolute future is not in human hands, precisely its hopeful expectation becomes the driving power in man's cultural activities: the Christian hopes through creating culture and vice versa. He fashions the future of the world by hoping for the absolute future. Or, to express it more cautiously: he ought to have this hope and thus also do cultural work. This includes a statement about an essential element of hope itself. This hope for eternity is realized in the constant transformation of the structures of secular life. Leaving aside the fact that "revolution" is a very vague and many-sided term, we might say:

Here Christian hope is declared to be the ground of an always revolutionary attitude of the Christian to the world. If Christianity be rightly understood and if Christians understand themselves correctly, things are exactly the opposite of what most Christians and non-Christians imagine: hope in the absolute future of God who is himself the eschatological salvation does not justify a fossilized conservatism which anxiously prefers the safe present to an unknown future; it is not a tranquillizing "opium for the people" in present sorrow; it is, on the contrary, the authoritative call to an ever-renewed, confident exodus from the present into the future, even in this world. Indeed, historical man does not realize even the ultimate transcendental structures of his nature in the abstract "interiority" of his own mind, but in communication with the world and his surroundings. And true "practice" in radical opposition to theory is not the mere execution of something planned and hence merely theoretical, but opening oneself to and risking the unplanned, so that the true possibility of what is risked appears only in this practice. True practice implies that the necessary and justifiable planning which manipulates the material world by technology, the human world by socialization and thus man himself, does not depreciate the insistent area of the unplanned. It does not reduce it to a defined residue merely waiting to be worked out. It rather increases the area in question and displays it more cleraly as the result of praxis itself, since man, as he breaks down the unforeseen data, builds up his own unforeseeable product. Hence in the practical risk of the unforeseen inner-worldly future man realizes his eschatological hope by looking away from himself to the absolute which is not in his power. It is therefore true that man must impress his hope on the structures of the world. This, of course, does not mean precisely that certain permanent structures of his secular world could ever be the permanent objectivation of his eschatological hope. On the contrary. Every structure of secular life both present and to come is called into question by hope, because this is the anticipation of what is not in our power, and the historical and social act of hope is realized in this calling into question, though not entirely.

For the Christian also accepts the passing away of the
"form of this world" in his individual life, in death and
the renunciation that anticipates death, and realizes his
hope even in them. This is anything but wild revolt. For
the spirit of revolt either elevates the immediate future
of the world into an absolute and thus is the opposite of
hope, namely a form of pride, or else it does not hope for
anything, but denies everything because it is not permanent, and thus is despair. But constant criticism also of the
secular structures is one of the forms of Christian hope.
For it does not hold on to anything in this life as if without
it man would fall into an absolute void; and at the moment
when he is becoming more clearly than before the master
of his world it orders him not only to let go what is taken
away from him, but also actively to surrender what, in
view of the infinite future of hope, he realizes to be transitory and thus replaceable even in time. It is strange that
we Christians who must take the radical risk of hope in
an absolute future should have acquired the reputation,
among others as well as among ourselves, that our principal virtue is the will to preserve the existing order. In
fact, however, the Christians as the pilgrim people of God
have been given the absolute command to hope, and this
includes that they must always abandon also fossilized
social structures. Theoretical faith cannot simply deduce
how the Christian is to realize this hope despite such ever
renewed exodus, and to what he clings (as is also possible)
because his hope takes away the semblance of the absolute
also from the temporal future. This concrete imperative
is not the result of the applied theory of the faith, just as
little as faith as such changes the general promise into a
special one which is grasped only by primeval hope. But
this hope commands individual Christians as well as Christendom to risk these ever new decisions between the

defence of the present and the exodus into the unforeseeable future. And hope can do this, for it has already done the greater thing. Through it man has abandoned himself into the eternal absolute over which he has no power. And in the power of this greater hope he also possesses the lesser hope, which is the courage to change the secular structures of his life, as the Council says. The greater hope is realized in the lesser, and eternal life in the creation of ever new forms of culture.

The Christian Character of the Secularized Ethos

We ought to be very careful in our judgment about the "secularization" of contemporary life. The plough and the sickle of former times were also secular objects. Today they have been replaced by tractors and treshing-machines, and thus there is not only a change in image and proportions, but there are also more objects in this world which can obstruct the religious view because they are so fascinating and so large. But they are there by rights, and as Christians we must simply accept the fact that there will be ever more man-made reality which is neither "numinous" nature nor is profane in the bad sense. To say it quite simply: the loaf of bread has become much bigger, thank God, but man can still realize that he does not live by bread alone, for he has always been tempted, not only now, to think the opposite. We make secularization only more dangerous if we dramatize it. And, let us be frank: is it really so certain that formerly, when religion and the Church played a greater part in public life, men really had more true faith, hope and charity, which, after all, are more important than anything else? God alone knows. The faith that is attacked by our secular world and is left to the free decision of the individual may well be more genuine. Further: is the seemingly secularized ethos of our time which speaks (and, let us hope, not only chatters) of the freedom and dignity of man, of responsibility and the love of one's neighbour, is this ethos a result of Christianity or not? It is its legitimate son, even though it is often a prodigal son who squanders his property far from his father's house. How could this ethos remain alive unless men still believed, even without admitting it, that they are children of God destined for eternal life? Is not this belief genuinely Christian, and could it remain alive at all apart from Christianity? And would this ethos still be so alive, indeed propagating itself, unless it were still living by the side of explicit Christianity? Surely the secularized ethos of our society receives its power from Christianity. Perhaps this, too, may be a case of living on the money of one's parents, but not wanting to admit that one did not earn it oneself. By the way, the United States is often regarded as a prime example of a secularized country. But on closer inspection we shall find that many heterogeneous elements do, indeed, exist there side by side, but that the Churches are nevertheless extraordinarily "present" in public life. Apart from the social services run by the state in which, after all, Christians have as much a share as every one else, it must be said that the participations of "humanists" in private charitable enterprises for the poor, the sick, neurotics, lepers, etc., is relatively modest. All honour to Albert Schweitzer, for example. But most private works of mercy, it seems to me, are done by practising Christians. Humanists attach too much importance to their own emancipation from Christianity and its "social power", and this prevents them from actual positive engagement. And finally, if we do not want the world to be submerged by a pagan secularism without God and without hope, we ought not to compile statistics and make forecasts, but should bear our Christian witness in the market place by word and deed. Everything else we can and must leave to God.

Is Christianity an "Absolute Religion"?

The Catholic Church is confronted by historical powers which she cannot neglect as being wholly "secular", but which are important for her, even though they are opposed to her. It is her duty to establish a relationship with them and to understand their existence insofar as she cannot simply approve of them. But she must bear the scandal of their opposition and conquer it by herself becoming the higher unity that embraces it. This is what is meant by "open Catholicism".

One of the most difficult elements of this pluralism is the multiplicity of religions which exists even after two thousand years of Christianity and its missionary activities. For no other religion claims to be *the* religion and the absolutely unique and only valid revelation of the one living God. Moreover, today the existence of many religions threatens the individual Christian more than ever before. For in the past another religion was at the same time also the religion of a different civilization, with which there were only very peripheral contacts, it was the religion of foreigners. Thus it is not surprising that the existence of such a religion should not have affected oneself at all.

Today the situation is very different. Everyone is everyone else's neighbour and therefore, whether willingly or unwillingly, conditioned by a communications system embracing the whole planet. Every religion has become a question and a possibility for every man; hence it challenges the absolute claim of one's own Christianity. We would therefore explain the basic characteristics of a dogmatic Catholic interpretation of the non-Christian religions, and thus help to solve the problem of the Christian position with regard to contemporary religious pluralism. We call it a dogmatic interpretation, because we consider the question not from the empirical point of view of the history of religions, but from the dogmatic standpoint of Christianity's own conception of itself.

We begin with the statement that Christianity claims to be the absolute religion destined for all men, which cannot tolerate any other as having equal rights beside it. This thesis is the basis for the Christian theological understanding of the other religions. Christ, the absolute Word of God, has come in the flesh and reconciled, that means united, the world to God through his death and resurrection, not only theoretically but in reality. Ever since, Christ and his permanent historical presence in the world which we call Church are *the* religion which binds man to God.

It should, however, be noted that Christianity has a historical beginning in Christ; but this means only that this absolute religion, too, must come to men historically, confronting and claiming them as their legitimate religion.

The question is therefore: Is the moment in time at which this absolute historical religion makes existentially real demands on men the same for all, or has the beginning of this moment itself a history and thus is not the same in time for all men, all civilizations and periods of history.

If we presuppose that our second theory is correct, this means that we can understand our first thesis in a more differentiated way. For we shall positively state only that

Christianity is meant to be the absolute and therefore unique religion of all mankind, but we leave open the question at which moment in time it is objectively binding for any man and any civilization. It should be noted that we are therefore concerned with the fact that a social entity is needed for salvation. Hence we may, indeed must, say without hesitation that this thesis implies that its social organization belongs to the very essence of religion.

Moreover, we may say that paganism continues to exist not because it has rejected Christianity, but because it has not yet met it in a sufficiently impressive encounter. If this is true, paganism will cease to exist in *this* sense, because the West has begun to enter the history of our whole planet. Or, to express it more cautiously, we enter an entirely new phase in world history, in which Christians and non-Christians, living in the same situation, confront each other dialogically.

Until the gospel actually enters the historical situation of a certain person, a non-Christian religion contains not only elements of a natural knowledge of God mixed with depravation caused by original sin and human elements, but also supernatural elements of grace. It can therefore be acknowledged to be a legitimate religion, even though in different graduations.

According to the first part of this thesis even non-Christian religions may be said *a priori* to contain supernatural elements of grace. This opinion is based on the theological principle that, as Christians, we must profess the dogma that God wills the salvation of all men even in the post-paradisal period of original sin. On the one hand this salvation is specifically Christian, for there is no salvation apart from Christ, while, on the other, God truly and seriously wants all men to be saved. Both can be combined only by saying that man is exposed to the influence of divine grace, which offers him communion with God, whether he accepts it or not.

The second part of our second thesis, however, goes further. It says that because of this the pre-Christian religions, too, need not simply be regarded as illegitimate but that they, too, can very well have a positive meaning. This applies also to religions which, in their concrete form, may contain many theoretical and practical errors. This is shown, for example, by a theological analysis of the structure of the Old Covenant. For in the Old Covenant such as it appeared in history there was much that was right and willed by God, but there were also a great many errors, wrong developments and depraved ideas, while there was no permanent infallible authority to separate the two. Hence we must give up the prejudiced idea that we may confront a non-Christian religion with the alternative of being either wholly of divine origin or a merely human thing. If in these religions, too, man is under grace, the individual must have the possibility of a genuine saving relation with God. Now man is a social being, and in earlier times he was even more radically involved in social ties. Hence it is unthinkable that he could have realized his relationship with God individually and interiorly, outside the actual religion which offered itself in the world around him. For, as has already been said, it belongs to the characteristics of a true, concrete religion that the individual religious practice is embedded in a social religious order. Hence the salvation God wanted man to have reached him according to the divine will and permission in the concrete religion of the historical conditions and circumstances of his life, though this did not deprive him of the right and the limited opportunity to criticize and to pay attention to the reforming impulses which God's providence always inspired in such a religion.

If this second thesis is correct, Christianity confronts an adherent of a non-Christian religion not only as a mere non-Christian, but also as a person who may already be regarded in certain respects as an anonymous Christian.

Now it must be possible to be not only an anonymous theist but, as has been said, an anonymous Christian. There is a twofold reason for this. For the man who becomes the "object" of the missionary activities of the Church may have approached and even found his salvation without having yet been reached by the preaching of the Church; and, secondly, this salvation which he has found must also be the salvation of Christ, because there is no other. And so it is true that in the last analysis the preaching of the Gospel does not make into a Christian a man absolutely forsaken by God and Christ, but that it transforms an anonymous Christian into a man who realizes his Christianity in the depth of his grace-endowed nature also objectively and in the communal confession of the Church.

This implies that this express self-realization of a formerly anonymous Christian is a higher phase of the development of this Christianity, demanded by his nature. Hence we may on no account conclude that the preaching of Christianity is superfluous, because a man is an anonymous Christian without it. For the self-realization of the formerly anonymous Christianity is demanded, first, by the incarnational and social structure of grace and Christianity, and, secondly, by the fact that a clearer and more reflected comprehension of Christianity offers a greater chance of salvation to the individual than his status as an anonymous Christian.

True, we cannot hope that religious pluralism will disappear in the foreseeable future; nevertheless, Christians themselves may well regard the non-Christian world as an anonymous Christendom. It follows, therefore, that today the Church will not so much regard herself as the exclusive community of candidates for salvation, but rather as the avant-garde, expressing historically and socially the hidden reality which, Christians hope, exists also outside her visible structure. The Church is not the community of those who possess God's grace as opposed to those who lack it, but the community of those who can confess explicitly what they and the others hope to be. Of course, this explicit confession and the historical institution of this salvation of Christ which is offered to all is itself a grace and part of salvation. The non-Christian may think it supercilious that the Christian attributes all that is good and whole in every man to the fruit of the grace of his Christ and regards the non-Christian as a Christian who has not yet found himself. But the Christian cannot do otherwise. And actually this seeming superiority is the way in which his greatest humility is expressed, both as regards himself and his Church. For it lets God be greater than both man and the Church. The Church will confront the non-Christian with the attitude of Paul who said: "What therefore you worship as unknown, this I proclaim to you." Hence we may well be tolerant and humble towards all non-Christian religions.

Visions

What I want to say here as a Catholic theologian does not concern particular visions and apparitions which have aroused popular interest, whether in the past or the present. It is quite outside my competence to be for or against any such individual event. I only want to make some remarks on the subject of apparitions and visions in general from the point of view of the theologian.

As a Catholic theologian I think that a Christian cannot deny the possibility of genuine visions, that is, of those produced by God and expressing his will, and also that he cannot say in principle that they concern only the visionary himself. For both the Old and the New Testaments testify to such events as caused by God and important for us. To accept only those described in Scripture and to reject all later ones altogether would mean abandoning both the Bible's and one's own credibility, whether we admit it or not. True, in Jesus Christ as the incarnate Word of God the history of God's self-revelation has entered its final eschatological phase, and everything necessary for salvation has been given us. But this does not exclude, it rather implies that prophecy and vision remain in the Church as an actualization of the permanent message of Christ.

The question of the nature of such visions is more difficult, for it involves criteria by which visions are to be distinguished from invented ones or those due to mere subjective human conditions. For there are also such, and they are probably the great majority, so that sober caution and the "examination of spirits" which Scripture recommends are indicated. For credulity causes more mischief than too much caution.

An authentic vision may probably be explained as a purely spiritual touch of God affecting the innermost centre of a man and spreading from there to all his faculties, his thought and imagination, which transform this touch. Hence, when a "vision" reaches the consciousness of the visionary it has already passed through the medium of his subjectivity, and therefore *also* bears his individual characteristics as regards language, interests, theological presuppositions and so forth. Hence the authentic vision is both divine and human, and because it is also human it is also affected by the visionary's nationality and the time in which he lives. In fact nothing else could be expected. It may well be assumed that in the case of a divinely caused vision of a heavenly person, too, though he or she appears to be there in the body, we have nevertheless to do with an imaginary vision, that means it is seen within the sphere of the interior imagination. This does not exclude that this vision is caused by an actual divine touch of the centre of the person (not merely by the visionary's own imagination) and that this touch is correctly translated into an imaginary picture. But Catholic theology does not offer a unanimous and binding opinion on this subject.

Where such visions are accompanied by prophecies and similar phenomena, these will best be explained in the same way as the comminatory texts of the Old and New Testaments. For precisely if they are genuine they do not anticipate future events, they are not phenomena of clairvoyance or second sight. Nor do they give detailed prescriptions for political action or offer an escape from unforeseeable history. They are also invariably conditioned by the visionary's own subjective experience. Such prophecies are calls to penance, perhaps in popular language, but touching many hearts. They can actually say only one thing, the same as the beginning of the gospel: Repent, believe the good tidings, "for the kingdom of God is at hand". Ultimately such prophecies cannot mean to say more if they are to be understood as actualizing the message of faith and not as fortune-telling. If they are wrongly interpreted they cease in any case to be true vision and prophecy for us.

These considerations also provide the criteria by which to distinguish genuine visions from the many false ones. Visions are authentic only if they are in accordance with Christ, if they conform to the teaching of the Church, serving not sensationalism but true Christian piety. They must lead to the centre of Christianity, not away from it to petty devotions and similar caricatures of biblical and ecclesial Christianity. Only then will they be true divine message and encounter. In judging these visions we shall, moreover, have also to take the whole character of the visionary into consideration. Finally, no Catholic Christian is bound to believe in any post-biblical vision unless he recognizes himself that it has its origin in God and is a call to his own free conscience.

Medical Ethics

We should not speak too easily of medical ethics unless we truly understand that objectivity is in itself a virtue. Objectivity is here defined as the capacity and will to see and admit objective facts, understood in this context as scientific data.

Though the physician's art is undoubtedly more than merely applied science, contemporary medical men are nevertheless right to base themselves on it, and insofar as they do so, they can and must be objective in their profession in the sense described above. Fortunately this objectivity seems to situate the medical art within a sphere which rarely requires decisions of conscience and the solution of ethical questions. It might be thought that an action will become less ethical the more "medical" it is, and medical problems of morality might be regarded as a sign that objectivity has not yet been carried far enough.

Even though the object is to determine as far as possible what the physician should do, nevertheless objectivity as the conscious will to be guided by the object rather than by prejudices (even by moral ones) is itself a moral attitude. No one finds it easy to adopt such a moral attitude which is determined by this "medical objectivity". For example: Any suppression of factors which are necessary for the clarity of a diagnosis but may be unpleasant for the physician contradicts not only the "object", but also objectivity as an ethical attitude, hence a "virtue of the physician". The content of medical activities is largely determined by medical, not by ethical principles; but the will to let one's actions be determined by objective medical principles is itself a moral action.

This becomes even more evident (I hope I may be forgiven the seemingly involved philosophizing) the more we realize that the principle of objectivity as such cannot be derived from the objects themselves, at least not in the sense in which it is used here. The objects can only determine conditional relationships. If such and such a weight is to be placed on a beam, its stability must correspond to the weight in question. Objects can determine the means, but not the end. If this or that disease is to be cured, such and such a medical method must be employed. But the medical "things" cannot tell the doctor *that* a man must be cured, if or that his life ought to be preserved, even in his old age, even when he no longer seems to be economically productive, even if to preserve his life is expensive. The medical data can only furnish a conditional principle of objectivity. The physician, however, who is more than merely a medical man, is guided by an absolute principle of objectivity which includes that something ought to be. Because of this, at least, the physician is also a moral person, the subject of an ethical imperative addressed to him, no matter to what he attributes this absolute principle.

This is the paradox of the whole medical situation. For the matter under discussion and which offers a conditional principle of conduct seems to militate against making this principle absolute. For whom does the physician encounter when he regards his patient only with the eyes of an objective medical scientist? To such a physician the patient might appear only too easily as perhaps a miserable human

being of whom one might doubt whether he was worth
keeping alive, who was himself biologically endangered
by his civilization, though without it he could not exist
even biologically. Thus the physician becomes involved in
ever increasing tensions between what he can achieve biologically and what he must achieve through man-made
civilization and its results.

Must such a human life be preserved as far as possible in
every case? Is the absolute demand that the physician
should defend the life of every man as far as at all possible
either the artificial and morally unreflected exaggeration
of the biological zest for life which rational man opposes
to the true "objectivity" of nature's action in life and
death, or is such absoluteness a genuine ethical demand?
This seems to me the fundamental ethical question which
every physician must answer, and actually does answer at
the sickbed. There will be many doctors who, in their practice, answer it in favour of the dignity of man, which is
more than mere biological zest for life. They will not,
however, reflect very much on what is the ultimate ground
of this dignity, which turns the conditional into an absolute principle, namely that the "object" which makes the
principle of objectivity an absolute principle is man, that is
the person. An explicit answer is given by the Christian,
for according to Christian teaching the dignity of man as
a person is founded on his relation to the absolute reality
of God. But every responsibly acting physician will give
an at least implicitly correct answer in which he reaches
an absolute ethic at least at one point.

The doctor is in a strange situation. He is a member of a
society in which there is a constant exchange of service and
remuneration. Nevertheless, as in the case of priests, artists
and perhaps even true politicians, more is required from
the physician than merely a paid service, namely his own

person and his ethics, which is part of his work. Because of his profession the physician is an advocate of the humane.

In the medical profession objective knowledge produces an achievement which can be paid for. But being a physician is not only a profession, but the vocation to be a man for others. As this vocation is lived in the sober unity of scientific knowledge and human achievement it is prevented from becoming mere humanitarian twaddle. Since members of the medical profession must be faithful to their vocation, their work will always be more than a mere way of earning their living, it will reveal true humaneness.

The Question of Justification Today

Today we Christians are all sadly conscious of the separation of the Christian Churches and of our duty to do everything in our power to heal the breach. This is a difficult task, because there are so many diverse reasons for the separations, reasons going back to the time of the reformation, reasons which have emerged only later through the historical development of the separated Churches, doctrinal reasons, but also sociological, national, cultural ones which by themselves do not add up to a real denominational difference. Then there are reasons which are subjectively felt as separating the Churches even though they no longer exist or may actually never have existed, reasons which would justify a pluralism within the one Church, but not a separation. All this is aggravated by the very fact that there are these separations, independent of their justification and the reasons which have led up to them. Because of this burden social and institutional history moves more slowly than we wish.

Because the reasons for the division between the Churches are so complex, there is no other way than to discuss each single cause by itself in order to remove or at least to weaken each obstacle to unity individually. It may seem that not much has been gained if a single obstacle has been intellectually overcome, for the other reasons are still there, and in reality we appear not to have progressed at all. But there is no other way. It is the same as in the case of a door which is fastened by ten nails. It is "more open" if even one nail has been extracted, for this will give us hope that we shall remove all, especially as our technical skill in drawing out the nails will also increase.

One of the decisive reasons for the separation of the Churches is the difference in the doctrine of man's justification before God through grace.

Here I cannot deal explicitly with the historical controversy, so I shall not discuss in detail the doctrine of the reformers, especially of Luther, nor the teaching of the Council of Trent on this point. Nor can I report the differences of the theological opinions which have since emerged on this subject in the various Churches. I also must leave aside the question why theologians on both sides could not agree, or at least thought they could not agree, about the subject of justification. All these questions cannot be treated here, and not only for reasons of time; for though they are very important for the history of theology, they lead into such a tangle of theological subtleties that they cannot be expected greatly to advance the ecumenical cause. Hence I should like to use another method. I want to say quite simply what a Catholic Christian thinks about justification, or, to express it more cautiously, what he is allowed to think. In my opinion this presentation will be acceptable to official Catholic doctrine which derives from the Council of Trent and need not be opposed either by contemporary Protestant Christians. This implies that the doctrine of justification, i.e. the *sola gratia*, is no reason for the separation of the Churches today. I must ask you to believe simply that my presentation is orthodox in the Catholic sense; whether it is also acceptable to Protestants must be decided by the Protestants themselves and their theologians. I do not pretend that my interpretation is the only one possible as regards points of view, formulations, emphases, etc. Considerable differences are possible and actually exist among Catholic theologians. But the same is the case in Protestant theology. Such theological differences need not destroy the unity of faith and confession, they need not be a cause for schism, and today neither side ought to emphasize them to such an extent as still to justify the separation of the Churches. Every single theological statement is only important and intelligible if it is considered within the whole complex of statements about justification. Hence every single statement can always be criticized, integrated, newly formulated and better protected from misunderstandings in the context of the whole. This has been only too often overlooked by both parties in their controversies. The object is infinite, while the aspects grasped by theologians and the terminology are finite and historically conditioned. Hence in the question of justification, too, we must simply take into account a theological pluralism which cannot be adequately abolished by a safe counter-argument.

First of all, we Catholics are as convinced as our separated brethren that today, too, the confession of the solely justifying grace of God is a fundamental truth of the Christian faith. In view of the central importance of this doctrine it matters less whether it is readily accepted by our contemporaries, provided that its message is not interpreted in a narrow, selfishly individualistic sense, but that the gracious divine act which opens man to God is from the beginning understood also as creating authentic community among men.

What we call salvation or justification is given to man, the creature and sinner, only through the free and undeserved grace of God, that is through God's free self-revelation in Jesus, the crucified and the risen Christ. Man's relation to God, which means his salvation, cannot be based on, or sustained by man's own initiative, but is instituted by the sovereign action of God. There are no "works" by which a man could render God "gracious" to himself, no initiative which would start with man. All saving activities of men are only a response, and even the very possibility and act of this response is once more based on God, who gives that we can and do accept his action.

God's grace must be accepted in freedom. Now this freedom which believingly accepts this grace is delivered by it from the finiteness and sinful egoism of the creature. Hence the Catholic doctrine of justification does not profess a semi-Pelagian synergism according to which salvation would be divided up into God's gracious act *and* the independent free act of man. On the contrary, man's free response to God is itself again the gift of God's grace.

This gift of God in which he communicates himself to sinful man is the "event" (not simply a constant dialectical state) through which the sinner becomes a justified man. God's grace truly reaches man, sanctifying him and making him a true heir of eternal life, that is he becomes something he was not before but now truly is. This statement, applied to the individual, does not autonomously fix the moment when this event takes place; but every man applies it to himself, not by reflecting on a certain empirical fact, but in the very act of faith and hope itself. Hence it does not mean that man absolves himself, but that he accepts in hope God's merciful judgment.

What God thus works in us and what we accept in faith and hope is the event which, while truly changing us "now", is yet wholly directed to the final judgment of God's mercy in which it will be perfected. Hence it is an event of promise which now is present only in hoping faith, but never becomes a possession which would be at our disposal in this world.

Though the various aspects and human developments of this grace-given event may be described in the scriptural terms of faith, hope and love, the event itself in its entirety can also be defined with St. Paul simply as "faith", and it may then be said that we are justified by faith and by faith alone.

Even though God's justifying grace truly affects and changes a man, and though it is seized in absolute hope and faith, nevertheless the event of justification does not happen only once by God's free action, but remains always dependent on his sovereign grace. It is inaccessible to a theoretical reflection which would abandon the hope of faith, and it leaves man under the threat of the world's power of sin. Moreover, a man can never absolve himself and decide with certainty whether his daily sins which he must acknowledge do not hide a radical No to God, even though he hopes that they do not exclude him from the kingdom of God. In this sense we Catholics, too, can and must speak of the sinner who is also just. (*Simul iustus et peccator,* according to Luther, Tr.) We must say that a man is justified only by always turning away from himself to the saving grace of God. The "state" of his justification is the possibility, offered by God, to do this over and over again.

This justifying grace of God frees us from the enslaving powers of death, from the merely external demands of the law and the world. It gives the children of God the power to act, it makes demands on them, indeed only the one demand that is founded on the love given by God, which man must answer by doing the work of love, producing the fruit of the spirit which is given to him. This work of responding love is valuable in itself because it is made possible by God, it is "wrought in God" (Jn 3:21). But just because of this it does not give man a claim on God, because it is itself God's gift to man if it is done in a love in which man sees only God and not himself. All praise of the objective dignity of the work of justified man can only be a praise of the truly creative grace of God. This grace vivifies truly, but crowns only its own work which it approves because it is done by itself as our freedom that has been set free.

I think that I have thus presented the Catholic doctrine of justification, briefly, it is true, but without having left out anything really essential. Of course, I could not interpret the many concepts and theses of the Council of Trent which are not simply intelligible and acceptable to a Protestant theologian. But I hope that the doctrine of justification need no longer separate us today. We have the duty rather to consider anew this "article" of the Christian faith so that it may be preached in a way that is credible to modern secular man. This is a much harder task than to produce agreement on this point among the separated Christians. For even if we are agreed on this question there remain many other obstacles to the unity of Christians in the one Church of Christ.

A Catholic Meditation on the Anniversary of the Reformation

It is difficult for a Catholic to speak on this subject. Ultimately he, like any other Christian, can only be silent before this event in the history of the Church. For it is caused by inevitable historical development as well as by intellectual, theological and social factors. There has been guilt on all sides, a guilt which is inexcusable, but nevertheless is always superseded by the mercy of God. And there has also been a necessity resulting from the freedom of historical decision, and which remains even when the situation and the freedom have changed into something quite different from what they were at the time. Of such historical events we must also say that they ought not to have happened, but that they are nevertheless included in the history of salvation, and though we have to regard them also as free decisions, we cannot positively imagine the alternative of what could, and ought to, have been but has not happened, namely the preservation of Christian unity combined with the necessary reform. Thus we might say all sorts of things about the reformation, but only to be finally silent before the mystery of God, who, in the end, is alone responsible and alone judges this history. But we are silent only because we hope that everything, and this also inevitably includes the guilt of the Church, is again the event of the greater love of God which has mercy on, and even through, the guilt.

However, if the Catholic must begin and end by saying that he cannot make a final statement on the Reformation, he must nevertheless voice some provisional opinions.

Even today the first point to be made must be the confession of guilt. Here the convinced Catholic especially is faced with a dreadful situation. He has not the right finally to judge those who at that time thought that their Christian conscience told them to break with the Church of the Papacy and to regard the Pope as the Anti-Christ who damaged the gospel of the grace of God by his very office (not only actually). The Catholic is also convinced that this principal concern of the Reformation is safeguarded in his own Church, indeed that this Church is its true and permanent home. He is firmly convinced that God has given us the duty to preserve the unity of the Church, regardless of whether through his forgiving grace he brings good even out of human disobedience. But though all this is true, and since one cannot simply detach oneself from one's Church, how can a Catholic not be horrified to realize that his Church, too, has a share in the guilt of the separation? Surely he must ask himself time and again—without finding an acceptable answer—how Alexander VI, Julius II and Leo X, the contemporaries of Luther, could have called themselves, in the Catholic view rightly, the Vicars of Christ and as such have been partly responsible for the catastrophe? How could he not realize that today, too, such things are possible, though in quite different forms, since they actually did happen in those days? And if he tries to gain an historical understanding of such things this will only increase his fear; for such understanding will only show how easily the Church, too, succumbs to the spirit of the times and becomes guilty without "noticing" it.

There is another point. The Catholic and his Church profess the *sola gratia* of the Reformers. God gives us in freely granted grace himself and his justice without any preceding "work" of ours. And if he wants us to accept this grace in responsible freedom, he must also grant by his undeserved grace that we accept it. There are good reasons why this basic event of God's free grace and its acceptance through grace should be called "faith", though this concept includes all the differentiated fullness of Christian existence which we call faith, hope and love; hence we Catholics, too, can agree to the *sola fide* of the Reformation. In my opinion every Catholic can agree to what bishop Lilje[1] has said on the subject. Both sides should be careful not to obscure this possible agreement by theological subtleties and secondary differences of opinion which may well be allowed to persist, and which exist also among Protestants. For such differences should not be allowed to justify existing separations which today have quite different reasons.

This, however, leaves us with the question why this was not understood at the time, why the reformers did not have the patience to listen to the ancient Church lovingly and understandingly till they heard this *sola gratia* and *sola fide,* and why the Church, on her part, did not speak more clearly and bravely about what was the just concern of the Reformers. Much might be said in explanation from the point of view of hermeneutics, philosophy and national and personal psychology. But in the end we shall be left with the incomprehensibility of history which has been discussed at the beginning.

Thirdly: the *sola scriptura* as a formal principle ought no longer to separate the Churches. The Catholic Church regards herself, according to Vatican II, as the servant of

---

[1] This chapter was originally written as an answer to an article by Bishop Lilje: "Reformation heute", *Stimmen der Zeit* 180 (1967), pp. 217—27.

Scripture. And the Protestant Christian knows that the New Testament originated in the apostolic kerygma of the living apostolic Church and therefore is and remains her book. He knows that Scripture receives its full meaning only through the preacher's actual interpretation, by which faith is awakened. Hence Scripture needs the Church to realize itself; it is not meant to be read only by oneself. Why then should we not be able to agree about the *sola scriptura*? Of course, this is possible only if permanent differences of opinion are not turned into principles of separation in order to justify existing facts.

On a fourth point I beg to differ from Bishop Lilje: The Catholic is not compelled by his faith to regard the Church and her magisterium as the first and fundamental factor of his Christian faith. No matter how his faith has originated psychologically, or how the interconnection of all its elements may be interpreted theologically, the Catholic believes the Church (not: in the Church), *because* he believes in God and his grace, in the crucified and risen Christ as his only Saviour, and not the other way round, even though as a Catholic he always believes in the "community of the faithful". Ultimately this fundamental decision is not supported by the Church and her magisterium, but these are supported by it; they are only a secondary norm for the contents of the individual Catholic's faith. The fundamental decision is, if one wants to call it that, the decision of the solitary conscience for which man is responsible to God alone. It is a decision for the Church, not one that is derived from the Church.

The Catholic understands this concept of the solitary conscience very well, provided it is not contaminated by modern individualism which diminishes man's stature and is, indeed, no longer regarded as his permanent inheritance. For today more than ever the experience of this conscience belongs also to the Catholic. True, we have the impression that this genuinely Christian concept of the reformers has been tainted by a subjectivism which was itself a product of the times; nevertheless, we Catholics should also admit that our quite legitimate defence of the authority of the magisterium has also been affected by paternalistic and feudalistic patterns through which this authority was, and perhaps even today quite often still is, presented to us.

The Christian is bound to hope against all hope, also in this matter. And thus he must hope that agreement among true Christians is possible also on the subject of the ministry, its necessity, its competence and its limitations. This hope, however, lays an obligation also on the authorities of the Catholic Church to be critical of themselves, to respect the conscience of every man which is responsible directly to God, and to avoid anything that may give the impression that the exercise of this ministry may have other purposes than the preservation of the one faith. The profession of this faith is necessary as an appeal to the conscience of the individual, who obeys because he is free in the greater community of the Church of truth, hope and love. Individual and community, conscience and authoritative doctrine, truth and institution will always be opposites which may cause incredibly bitter conflicts. Yet they ought never to be divorced from each other, else each would be destroyed precisely when it thinks it has conquered the other.

But even if we are thus reconciled in the "idea", this does not mean that the actual separated Churches are united, those Churches which for 450 years have lived side by side, fighting and contradicting each other, or, worst of all, indifferent to one another. We should thank God that we are at least no longer indifferent, but that theologians on both sides have once more begun to learn

from each other and that we have all realized more intensely the duty to seek the ecclesial unity of Christians,
because it is the inexorable demand of the Lord of the
Church. Nevertheless, it seems to me that even today none
of the Churches has as yet that will to unity which they
all ought to have. Separation is still considered a natural
fact which must be presupposed.

I do not think that the leaders of the Churches are really
wholly devoted to the cause of ecumenism. Today, when
Christendom is in mortal danger, the Churches ought
surely to be prepared to make even now any concessions
to each other that are not absolutely contrary to their
convictions. Within these limits the courage to take risks
is the only possible tutiorism. There are still enough differences on all sides which, on strict examination, will prove
to be not necessarily causes of separation and which ought
to be proclaimed unimportant, whether they concern canon
law, the liturgy, the way of life, administration or theology. All parties are still subconsciously far too inclined to
justify actual divisions theologically.

We Catholics have received a theoretical programme for
a new evaluation of our dogmas in Vatican II's teaching on
the "hierarchy of truths", but this programme is still far
from being carried out in practice. For we do quietly
presuppose that unless a doctrinal agreement is reached
on the basis of the present formulation of doctrine and
within its perspectives, we shall cease to be Catholics. We
actually do not have sufficient hope and courage to develop the controversial points of doctrine in such a way
that they can become intelligible and acceptable for the
others, or at least need no longer be regarded as separating
the Churches. We have not yet asked ourselves sufficiently
whether everything the Latin Roman Church has proclaimed as her dogma must be accepted by those Christians

who are to join us with the same formulas, emphases and perspectives. If we believe that in the future, too, the Church of Christ will be the Roman Catholic Church, this does not mean that this Church of the future will be exactly the same as the Catholic Church is now, and especially as it now appears to outsiders.

But are we really working for our Church of the future, not with wildly revolutionary methods, but with creative imagination and courage, patiently accepting also what has historically grown? I dare not affirm that we all work sufficiently for her according to our calling. The true Church above all has the duty to "give way" wherever her faith permits it. But does she do this sufficiently? And does she do it without regard to prestige and mere custom, without expecting advance payments from the other side, even risking to be misunderstood, simply in the evangelical folly of love? Is she already making room for all the differences that may legitimately be expected from past and future history, or does she still in parts consider desirable that uniformity which has been her right and her destiny in the time which is now coming to an end? Surely we Catholics do not yet collaborate with all other Christians as much as we might to bear witness to the gospel by sacrifice and love. In the missions especially this could be done much more effectively if only the theorists would get more creative ideas about such possibilities. We must leave it to the Protestant Christians to decide whether they, too, have to face similar questions; in any case, we Catholics must practise self-criticism.

We Catholics, however, should like to be allowed to ask one pertinent question about the whole problem of ecumenism, not in order to manoeuvre the other side into an unfavourable position, but because it simply cannot be avoided. We must ask who is to speak authoritatively for the Protestant partner in the ecumenical dialogue. For what power and authority do the official leaders of the Protestant Churches possess in order to discuss, in the name of their communities, a desirable doctrinal unity in such a way that we may hope for its realization? We understand very well—at least I hope we do—that owing to the principles of Protestantism this question is difficult to answer. But surely it must be posed if an ecumenical dialogue is to be more than merely private theological conversations between individuals. May we Catholics hope that in the Protestant Churches there is a growing understanding for the concept of "Church" and of authoritative teaching together with the courage also to define and limit? If such a development were to take place there would then also be an official partner who could say authoritatively what does or does not separate us, and who could expect a large following. During the Third Reich the Evangelical Church of Germany had the courage to speak authoritatively and to condemn the "German-Christians". It refused to accept any who belonged to this organization as Christians on the same terms as its own members. Today these Protestants will no doubt say that this was a charisma which could or should not be institutionalized. We Catholics can only hope that such a charismatic Yes to the Catholic Church of the future may be given from above, and that the Spirit may then work also through the institution and not only in spite of it, simply because this is inevitable.

This leads to another question. On both sides we are not the same as we were 450 years ago, and this gives us new hope. But it involves also new difficulties which cannot yet be fathomed. We should state quite frankly, especially if we take the "hierarchy of Christian truths" seriously, that the doctrinal differences which divide the modern

Protestant Churches are much deeper and more radical than those that separated the original Protestant denominations from the Tridentine confession. While Protestant Christians are convinced that, for the sake of their faith and conscience, they may not be joined to us in the same Church and Eucharist, they yet do not have the same difficulties with regard to those of their fellow Christians in whose theology hardly anything is left of the ancient creeds of the Reformers. I know that the matter is not simple. The "orthodox" Protestant may say that he tolerates radical heresies in his Church only for the sake of freedom of conscience and teaching, but that they are not for this reason part of the official creed of his Church, while that of the Catholic Church includes doctrines which he must reject in conscience, even if it were only the doctrine of the infallibility of the Pope or perhaps a Marian dogma. But may we not ask such an "orthodox" Protestant whether his Church might not, after all, practise such tolerance which, existentially and ecclesially, would not be distinguishable from a recognition, even if it were not expressed by the authorities in so many words? Surely we may ask him whether his view of the Church, too, must not include doctrines that ought not even to be tolerated in the Church if she is to have one confession and not to degenerate into a mere external religious organization. Can one be sure of a unity of confession if all conceptual statements are regarded as mere optional interpretations (*Interpretamente*), while what is actually meant lies beyond and cannot be expressed at all? Surely we Catholics should be allowed to hope that the Protestant Churches may one day be given grace and courage to achieve a greater unity of doctrine so that they will become better partners in the ecumenical dialogue.

I do not think that such a hope should be interpreted as

the supercilious pride of those in happy possession. Indeed, we Catholics have no reason whatever for such a pride. An authoritative magisterium would be of no use to the Catholic Church if there were no freely given obedience to it. So the actual situation of personal faith may be the same in the Catholic Church as in Protestantism, though it is hidden behind the façade of the official doctrine (though we do not dispute that this is also of theological importance).

Thus we come to the new common task shared by all Christian Churches of our time, namely that they all must bear witness to God, his Christ and his grace in a world that does not want to hear their message and that they all have the duty to proclaim it in such a way as not to make it unintelligible or incredible. Today we recognize each other more clearly than formerly as Christians in a theological, not only in a sociological sense. This implies that, by the grace of God, we still have a common faith which is not destroyed by doctrinal differences, however important. We have not the right to judge each other saying: because you believe or reject such and such a thing, what we still have in common is merely verbal. We must and can bear a common witness before the world. We must say it in a new way, because the world and we, it is to be hoped, with it, have changed. Hence we have the right and the duty to think about this new task, and Bishop Lilje is right in saying that in a certain sense the old doctrinal differences have been relativized. Even those Catholics most devoted to the Pope must realize today that it is infinitely more important to tell the world credibly what is actually meant by "God" (which in former times could simply be presupposed) than to indulge in controversy about the First Vatican Council.

Perhaps this new common task will be the best way of

progressing in the ecumenical dialogue. Faced with this frighteningly serious task the Churches, without losing their true inheritance, may yet change so much that they will one day be able to say in blissful surprise: we may celebrate the Supper of our one Lord together in the same faith, hope and love, we may announce God's mercy to the whole world as the one small flock of Christ and we may together expect the coming of God's kingdom. May this day dawn before the end; but it is solely the gift of God's grace. But such is also the task which we must acknowledge to be ours and accept with courage, faith, prayer and ecclesial self-denial. Only he looks truly back into the past who looks forward to the future and to our common Lord, who takes pity on our guilty past and offers us a future in his grace.

V. FREE ACCEPTANCE OF
CREATURELINESS AND CROSS

"Remember, Man, that You are Dust"

It seems to me that contemporary artists and writers are more interested in truth than in beauty, if the latter is understood in the traditional sense. They speak more than heretofore about the unredeemed misery of our existence; they say that we are dust and ashes and return to dust, tired wanderers on dusty roads going where? We do not know. All amusements seem almost to be only a façade hiding anything but a natural *joie de vivre*. Is it then still necessary that we should gather here to be signed with a cross of ashes and to be told: Remember, man, that you are dust and will return to dust? Is it still necessary to commemorate the death of the Lord, wich is only too present to us in our own life and in every mortal man, in whom we encounter Christ according to his own words? Yes, indeed, "It is right and fitting", as we say in the Preface of the Mass. But there is a difference whether we proclaim our own misery or whether we let Christ tell us about it in the words of the Church. For if we say it ourselves it is almost inevitable that we should either protest against it or indulge in self-pity; at best we shall be at a loss, not knowing what to do about it all.

It makes a difference whether we mourn for ourselves or whether another is mourning for us. The latter comes very near to being a genuine comfort: true, our misery is not

taken from us, on the contrary, the other says, with almost
cruel directness that we are ourselves dust and ashes.
But he who mourns with us has taken them into his very
heart.

This mourning of Christ and the Church on our behalf
means, first of all, that we are allowed to mourn, for our
sorrow has not yet been overcome, neither by our own
strength nor by the comforting of another. It means further
that we are allowed to weep, we need not pretend that we
can get over everything keeping a stiff upper lip, we may
well be completely bewildered, unable to produce a harmony out of all the contradictions and dissonances of our
life. For God alone can do this, and we ought not to pretend that we, too, could do the same. But if we entrust
ourselves completely to the ineffable mystery of our God
we shall not, indeed, be freed from our bewilderment; on
the contrary, this will fall into the holy darkness in which
it will become almost more cruelly painful than before.
Nevertheless, there is no other way to dissolve it; it is still
falling and has not yet been dissolved, therefore we are
allowed to mourn.

The sorrow of Christ joins our sorrow and says: Your
mourning is mine. In the darkness of death I cried out: My
God, my God, why hast thou forsaken me? But before that
I had said—an incomprehensible mystery—Father, into
thy hands I commend my life. Do not say that it was easier
for me to mourn, because I was also God. I was and I am
a man like you. True, I was the man in whom the Word of
God had made humanity his own; but because of this absolute nearness I was also more exposed than anyone else, I
could experience more poignantly what it means to be a
man, who is not God. And how can you know what happens when God's omnipotent love takes the misery of his
creature to his own heart and lets it penetrate even into the

centre of this heart? How do you know what happens when his omnipotent love compels the ever-blessed God to suffer the misery of the creature as his own? Your sorrow is my own sorrow, thus says the voice of Christ in the words of the Church today.

But in thus mourning with us Christ and the Church are also asking us if we hear and accept the accusation underlying this mourning. Not all, but much of what we call our pain ought to be called our guilt. We cannot separate our guiltless torment from the torturing guilt in which we have involved ourselves. We are always experiencing the one pain in which our own guilt also calls to us, the guilt of unredeemed lust and rebellious despair. Hence, while sorrowing we also always accuse ourselves. And if Christ sorrows with us, he does not relieve us of the accusation which we should level against ourselves, if we would only understand our sorrow correctly.

The words said to us on Ash Wednesday as our truth, our comfort and our indictment are written in Scripture at the beginning of the history of mankind; they are a statement and a judgment of what man is from the beginning. These words concern a beginning, but they are said by God. They sound like a statement about our future, about the abyss of death into which we shall fall. But our future is not what is said to us in these words, so that we should know whence we come and what we must endure, our future is he who says these words; their deepest sense is that HE is addressing us. He speaks to us because he wants to be involved with us. He has not yet finished speaking, he will have done so only at the end, when he will have fully communicated himself. In hard words he reveals to us the abyss of our origin, in order to promise us himself as the abyss of our future. He is ours, this is our expectation and our hope against all hope. The future is different from the past, else it would not be future. But there is future because there is hope.

What has just been said about the meaning of the Ash Wednesday words could not have been said otherwise; yet all this will remain empty talk unless everyone applies it to himself, changing the general into the particular, for only thus can these words be realized in the individual life. Thus death will perhaps mean only the quiet patience with which we endure the boring daily round, a request for pardon and its granting; perhaps it means the patience with which we listen to, and bear with another, or the unrequited faithfulness of love. Such death may also mean that we overcome our irritation with someone we find uncongenial, or that we have the courage of our convictions without being accorded the esteem that often goes with it; it may mean being faithful to one's own vocation even though this may not be popular at the moment. Nevertheless, all this is only a "meaning"—the words still remain general and carry no obligation. They can be made binding only by the action of one's own heart, for this alone creates reality, eternity in time. For all these ordinary daily actions of a decent person really involve a death, namely the silent, unsung relinquishing of oneself and of the blind desire for felt happiness which is so unrewarded that we only experience it as just part of the daily round and cannot even savour it as an action that is its own reward. We die throughout our life. What matters is if we do it willingly, if the Passion of Christ is also our own deed through which we receive grace.

The Passion of the Son of Man

Words for Holy Week

I

If we want truly to be Christians, this week ought to be a time when we share in a special way in the Passion of Christ. We do this not so much by indulging in pious feelings, but by bearing the burdens of our life with simple fortitude and without ostentation. For we share by faith in the Passion of our Lord precisely by realizing that our life is a participation in his destiny. We find this difficult, because so often we fail to understand that the bitterness and burden of our own life do—or should—give us a mysterious share in the destiny of all men. Internal and external distress carries the deadly danger of egoism, because it tempts a man to think only of himself, to be only concerned with his own affairs and thus to increase his distress by his self-centred loneliness in a vicious circle. But it should, and it can be different. We can freely accept our own distress as our contribution to the destiny of all men, whose burdens are thus mysteriously lightened. This can be verified in everyday life. The person who suffers selfishly, who rebels and complains, actually seeks to transfer his own burden to others, instead of bearing it silently so that it may be easier for them. But this is only the commonplace appearance of a more profound, all-pervading law: We always bear also the burden of others, and we should know that they, too, bear our burden in a thousand different ways which we do not know at all, beyond the restrictions of time and space to the very limits of human history. Or have we never been terrified because the whole sorrow and torment of mankind seemed to confront us in a seemingly insignificant experience, in a tormented child, in a beggar or a dying man? And did not this sorrow seem to invite us to recognize it as our own and to help to bear it, and to accept our own sorrow in such a way that all mankind's sufferings would be made more bearable and be redeemed? If we were aware of this, we would also better understand that we can share in the Passion of the Son of Man during this Holy Week, we would understand that his Passion is the unique acceptance of the passion of mankind, in which it is accepted, suffered, redeemed and freed into the mystery of God.

II

In Holy Week we often speak of the passion, the cross and the death of Jesus. But this passion confronts us even, indeed first of all, in our practical life, not only in our pious thoughts. This can be obscured both by the mysterious horror of the cross itself and by the fact that we have become too familiar with the language in which it is expressed. Today we still speak of the cross only in the explicit language of the Church and religion; perhaps some pious old Christians may still use the expression for the experience of their own life. This linguistic change makes it more difficult to relate our own life to the Passion of the

Lord. But what do we mean when we speak of the cross, the passion, of death in relation to Jesus? In him these words had certainly a very deep and mysterious meaning. Nevertheless, the Son of Man, too, experienced them as we do, only today we use different expressions. What is meant by them does not only take place in those moments when the incomprehensibility of life can no longer be shirked, for example, when our dearest die, when a lifelong love is for ever destroyed by unfaithfulness, when the doctor tells us that death is imminent and inevitable. What is meant is always present, especially if we do not want to admit it, if we suppress it and cover it over. It is always there: in the mute presence of death throughout our life, in the loneliness which is there even when we are quite near to our beloved, in the colourless daily round, in the thankless performance of our duty selfishly exploited by others, in the fatigue and deterioration of our life, which was once so marvellously colourful and exuberant. This passion and death are present when the inner voice through which a man had expressed himself has ceased to make itself heard and when all our life and all our hopes have ended in inevitable disappointment. We ought to allow our living experience once more to fill the empty verbal shells of an all-too-familiar religious language, so that the word of the cross and of the imitation of the crucified Lord might suddenly receive an intelligible content and a power that force men to make a decision. Then we would know that we must truly act out our faith when we are asked: Do you accept the cross of your life, do you know that it means sharing in the Passion of the Lord? Then we would meet not only in the liturgy of the Church but in our very life the words: Hail, Cross, our only hope in this Passiontide, the passion that is also ever present and is always suffered even in the most commonplace life.

III

The car in which we ride through life may seem to us a fine, comfortable caravan which takes us on a holiday trip though beautiful scenery. But it is also the prison van of our finite being, in which we are shut up with our disappointments and the misery of our boring daily life, in which we ride on to our final end, which is death. We all are cross-bearers in the sober sense which we have discussed above. No one can rid himself of this cross of existence. But precisely for this reason it is difficult to know whether we accept this cross in faith, hope and love to our salvation, or whether we only bear it protesting secretly, because we cannot free ourselves from it but are nailed to it like the robber on the left of Jesus, who cursed his fate and blasphemed the crucified Lord by his side. It is almost impossible to distinguish and decide between these two attitudes. And yet all depends on this distinction. Everything—that is the meaning which we give to our life or rather which we allow God to give it, and thus our salvation. The one question is whether we accept it or not. When do we accept it? Certainly not if we talk much about it and imagine ourselves very brave. Certainly not by exaggerating the little sorrows of our daily life and whining and whimpering about them. Certainly not if we imagine that the will to bear the cross prevents us from defending ourselves and from leading a free, healthy and sound life as long as is at all possible. Nor does the word of the cross allow us to be indifferent to the cross of another and only interested in our own comfort. But to accept the cross does not mean either that we should take a perverse pleasure in pain or be so dulled that we no longer feel it. But in what, then, does this acceptance consist? It is difficult to say, because it can take so many forms that a common factor is scarcely noticeable. It may appear as a brave will to fight on, as sober patience, a heroic love of the cross, uncomplaining sharing in the fate of others, self-forgetfulness in the sorrows of one's neighbour and in many other forms. It seems to me that the crucified Lord has fathomed all these forms when he cried out on the cross: My God, my God, why hast thou forsaken me? and when he prayed: Father, into thy hands I commend my life. In the first quotation the cross remains incomprehensible and is not explained away, while in the second it is accepted as this remaining mystery. Both together constitute the truth of the acceptance. The whole may be present even if we only utter the first cry while the second is there, though it remains unspoken. Whether or not we become wholly dumb when death takes away our voice, that is perhaps the last mystery of our life.

IV

On Maundy Thursday Christendom commemorates the institution of the Eucharist by our Lord. It happened in the night he was betrayed. Ever since then Christians have celebrated this meal despite all their divisions, though in sorrow that they cannot all celebrate it together. Nevertheless, it is a consolation that all who call themselves Christians do celebrate it, even though their interpretation of what happens at it is not everywhere quite the same. The meaning of the sacred meal is immensely wide and diversified. We gather round a table, the altar, confessing by this very fact that we are to be united in love like a family. We know by faith that the Lord has promised to be present in such a congregation and is mysteriously there among those who share the meal. His death is proclaimed until he comes again, the death which brings us forgiveness and life, but which also takes us, who die throughout our life, into its incomprehensible mystery and melancholy. But the meal that is celebrated is already filled with the blessed joy of eternal life which we hope for and expect. Christ unites us in the Church, the community of those who believe and love, which is his body, by giving himself to us in the elements of bread and wine, the perfect signs of his body and blood. In this meal the word God speaks to us, the word of eternal love becomes radiantly present in our darkness. In this sacrifice Christ, who has given himself for us once and for all, is presented as the Church's gift to the eternal God.

Now it is true that, from God's point of view, the liturgical celebration of this sacred meal contains what it signifies and gives what it says. Nevertheless, as far as we are concerned, it receives its ultimate truth and fulfilment only when it is celebrated as that "communion" which takes place in the daily round of our earthly life. Even in the Eucharist Christ becomes our salvation rather than our judgment only if we also recognize him in the least of our brothers whom we meet in ordinary life. We announce the death of the Lord in the Mass to our salvation only if in serene faith and hope we also encounter it in its everyday form of sorrow and disappointment. This is how we must live if the Eucharist is to be our salvation and not our judgment. But this awesome truth contains also a blessed mystery: Many may perhaps meet the Lord in their daily life by faithfully obeying the transforming voice of their conscience even though they have not yet found the holy table of the Church where he celebrates his sacred meal with us.

V

The day we are commemorating seems far away, yet actually it did not begin in history and has never come to an end. For it began with history itself and is still present in our own life today. For what finally comes to light in the darkness of the first Good Friday is, in the words of St. Paul, the ever-valid and ever-new scandal and folly of the cross, though the apostle adds at once that just this is the wisdom and power of God for those who believe. True, we do not always feel this. It is even a good thing that we realize our condition only rarely, else we should not be able to bear it. But on this Good Friday we ought to consider of our own free will the terrors of life, so that we may stand fast when we must face the abyss and endure it. For we all are gathered round the cross of the Crucified, whether we look up to him or try to look past him, whether we are at the moment quite gay and happy (this is not forbidden) or frightened to death. We are standing under the cross, being ourselves delivered to death, imprisoned in guilt, disappointed, deficient in love, selfish and cowardly, suffering through ourselves, through others, through life itself, which we do not understand. Of course, if we are just quite comfortable we protest against such pessimistic outlook which wants to take away our joy in life (which is quite untrue); when we are vigorous in body and soul we refuse to believe that this will not last for ever. Yet we are always under the cross. Would it not therefore be a good thing to look up to him whom they have pierced, as Scripture expresses it? Ought we not to admit what we have suppressed and to *want* to stand where we actually do stand? Surely we ought to have the courage to let our heart be seized by God's grace and to accept the scandal and absurdity of our inescapable situation as "the power of God and the wisdom of God" by looking up at the Crucified and entering into the mystery of his death. Many certainly do this without being aware of it by their way of life which accepts death in silent obedience. But we may also fail to do this. Hence it is better expressly to celebrate the Good Friday of the Lord by approaching his cross and speaking his last words with him. They are quite simple, everyone can understand and say them with him. This is the abyss of existence into which we fall. And we believe that there dwell love and life themselves. We say Father, into your hands I commend myself, my spirit, my life and my death. We have done all we could do—the other, the ineffable that is salvation will come too.

VI

Holy Saturday is a strange day, mysterious and silent. It is a day without a liturgy. This is as it were a symbol of everyday life which is a mean between the abysmal terror of Good Friday and the exuberant joy of Easter. For ordinary life is also mostly in-between the two, in the centre which is also a transition and can only be this. Perhaps the worst in life is already behind us. Though this is not certain, and perhaps not even radically true. For the very end is still before us. Nevertheless, may be we have "come through"; perhaps the old wounds are no longer bleeding, we have become wiser and more modest in our desires, we expect less from ourselves and others, and our resignation is not too painful. This may be just as well. We cannot always have everything in one exercise, as a medieval mystic says. We need not always be horrified by the incomprehensibility of life nor entranced by its glory, we need not always celebrate the highest liturgy of life or death. Ordi-

nariness, too, may be a blessing. But this ordinariness of
the in-between must be understood as a transition, the
transition from Good Friday to Easter. Man, especially the
Christian, has not the right to be modest, he must maintain
his infinite claim. The fact that his pain is bearable must
not be allowed to replace his blessed duty to hope for the
infinite joy of eternity. Because God *is*, he may demand all,
for he is all. Because death has died in Christ, our resignation must also die. The Holy Saturday of our life must be
the preparation for Easter, the persistent hope for the final
glory of God. If we live the Holy Saturday of our existence
properly, this will not be a merely ideological addition to
this common life as the mean between its contraries. It is
realized in what makes our everyday life specifically
human: in the patience that can wait, in the sense of hu-
mour which does not take things too seriously, in being
prepared to let others be first, in the courage which always
seeks for a way out of the difficulties. The virtue of our
daily life is the hope which does what is possible and expects God to do the impossible. To express it somewhat
paradoxically, but nevertheless seriously: the worst has
actually already happened; we exist, and even death cannot deprive us of this. Now is the Holy Saturday of our
ordinary life, but there will also be Easter, our true and
eternal life.

Institutional Spirituality of the Church and Personal Piety

Today the consciousness of the Church's theoretical and practical faith certainly undergoes a necessary change which should in itself be welcomed. For the institutional forms, often supported by non-theological factors, which have favoured an almost unquestioning popular religious practice, are losing much of their inner force. Thus a truly personal faith is demanded much more decisively than formerly. No doubt this change gives the Christian faith the chance to be realized in absolute freedom, which corresponds indeed to its inmost nature; but, on the other hand, the dangers inherent in it ought not to be underestimated. To speak of a "Church of the congregation" *(Gemeindekirche)*, as distinct from the established Church *(Volkskirche)*, is not unobjectionable. One danger at least is that of a onesidedly "personalistic" conception of the faith which neglects the institutional forms of the Church's life. The following considerations attempt to make a modest contribution to the solution of this problem.

Every existing form of piety presented to my choice, as it were, from outside, may be considered under the aspect of the externally inflicted law. It matters comparatively little whether this is strictly a commandment of God or the Church, or only a custom, a tradition or suchlike. All these things agree in this that they confront me with something which is already there, that they at least appear to limit my spirituality which is obviously the most intimate realization of my freedom. Now if personal freedom is basically a unique gift of God, what we call spirituality must have an inner connection with it. Hence the institutional norms of the Church and the freedom which is realized most decisively in the spiritual life cannot be in complete mutual harmony from the beginning.

Freedom Related to the Situation

First of all it must be stated that in Catholicism there is certainly something like a will to the law, even within the sphere of piety. However, as a social being man lives necessarily in community, and though he is the subject of radical freedom, he is yet not its abstract subject, confronted, as it were, with the variety of its indifferent possibilities. Even where we act in our innermost being, claiming the ultimate freedom of committing ourselves we act always within a pre-existing sphere. We are given a certain time which is not of our choice, we have inherited a certain psychological make-up, or we are placed within a definite historical situation. Hence freedom cannot ultimately consist in retiring into a sphere not affected by all these given conditions, nor can it be realized in mere opposition to them. I can only protest against what exists, not for example, against the government of a Herod III or Herod IV. In other words, whether we protest or revolt—and even revolution can be necessary, indeed it can be the sacred duty of a Christian in certain circumstances—we are always still imprisoned within our own concrete situation. The essence of freedom, therefore, may also consist in accepting given conditions in order slowly to change them. Thus—however the philosophers of history from the Stoics to Nietzsche may explain it—there must be such a thing as *amor fati* in its proper sense in which freedom finds its innermost essence. This may also be rightly applied to the social and historical ecclesial conditions of Christian piety insofar as this is realized in freedom.

The Norm as Freedom's Way to Itself

Moreover, we are not simply free but must become so. That truth which is mine and which comes wholly from within is not yet simply what I have only accepted in the formal freedom of Yes or No. I am only on the way to this my actual truth and it is the work of a lifetime to find and accept myself in freedom. For I suppress much of my actual truth, I do not want to admit it; I am perhaps in an ultimate attitude of protest without noticing it; despite all my talk about the love of one's neighbour I may even be the greatest egoist without realizing it. All I am meant to become may perhaps appear to me as rigid legalism. I can therefore achieve my true freedom only by a change in my given personality which delivers it from the selfishness in which it is imprisoned. And this may be applied also to the piety which appears as legalistic. Hence even in the realm of piety there must be a will to the law.

All those fastings laws, religious customs, devotions (which I may perhaps hate) and whatever else belongs to parish life and hits me as "law" is not necessarily wrong only because I reject it in a protest which is very problematical. Perhaps I may not even have understood some of these things, perhaps they are simply demanded by love for the others, for the Church, which means a certain member of the Church at a certain point of time.

What we should like to emphasize is this: There is a right institutional and legal piety which rightly makes demands on us in the ecclesiastical regulations about the liturgy, fasting, Sunday Mass, etc. It is by no means clear that only that form of the Mass is most marvellous and personally most authentic which disregards all the precepts of the Church including those of the Second Vatican Council. This is no vindication of Christian freedom, however strongly some people may believe it to be.

Christian Spirituality as Permanently Dependent on its Own History

The whole heritage of the Christian tradition of spirituality belongs, of course, also to this institutional material which is offered as a possibility or even as a demand. Why should we replace a two thousand year old Christian practice of meditation and asceticism by what we have read somewhere about Zen Buddhism and Yoga? It is certainly a rewarding task to synthesize Eastern and Christian piety and asceticism. But it is surely naive to esteem *a priori* psychotherapy and the practices of Yoga more highly than the traditional Christian devotions. If a person does not understand or like the rosary, for example, he is perfectly free, as a Christian, not to say it; yet for me it is a very wonderful thing, and it is my own private experience that it is said also by people of whom one would not believe it. There are, of course, also many literary treasures of spirituality, for example even today we may well recommend reading St. Augustine, St. John of the Cross, Teresa of Avila or any well-edited selection of mystical texts.

Certainly, modern critical exegesis is necessary and valuable. But the light of God and the Holy Spirit were active in the Church long before biblical criticism. A true theologian ought to prove his education also by planning within five or ten years to acquire an idea of the history of spirituality by reading Gregory of Nyssa, Augustine, the great medieval mystics, Francis de Sales or Bérulle and Charles de Foucauld, to mention only a few names. A true piety which respects the "law" might well be occupied also in this way.

The Free Acceptance of a Spiritual Order

We must, moreover, consider what I should like to call self-appointed institutional piety. Spirituality is impossible without a certain order, and this applies to lay people as well as to nuns and Jesuits brought up on the Ignatian Exercises. True spirituality does not consist in pious feelings, because we are perhaps just now in love or have some sorrow. This is at best a foretaste of the real thing, which must bear fruit in a truly personal decision affecting the whole life. This means, to use a provocative expression, that there must be a certain system in the spiritual life. It may be quite modest, corresponding to the daily life of the individual, and can be very different for the parish priest or the layman from what it is in a religious house. It may also be quite different from the spiritual system of the Third Orders or the Marian Congregations. The details do not matter, what is important is that there can be no vigorous spirituality without discipline, without a certain hardness against oneself, without a plan, without making demands on oneself also in the religious sphere and if one does not feel like it at the moment. Every Buddhist monk would laugh at us if we thought these things were unnecessary for the serious practice of spirituality. It would be the same as if somebody wanted to become a professional pianist without practising ten hours each day for six or eight years. How far we shall advance depends on God and our own life. But even though we may have to endure a spiritual odyssey and may meet many unexpected obstacles, we ought to make a little more progress than those who have merely been indoctrinated with a little external Christianity which expressed itself merely in a bored attendance at Sunday Mass, perhaps an Easter confession and the receiving of the last sacraments.

Evidently intellectuals are no better men only because they are educated; this shows itself especially in the case of theologians, no matter whether they are priests or laymen, who have chosen theology and spirituality as their profession or even as their intellectual hobby. Surely, even outside the sphere of theoretical reflection we ought to achieve a little more than a Christian life that is content with observing the rules. But actually we intellectuals, too, have not progressed much further in our faith. Indeed, we are perhaps in greater danger, because we think that our theorizing is the same as a true Christian life of prayer, faith, self-denial and humility. Moreover, we may be less truly Christian than the so-called "simple Catholics" of the Christian "people", if only because the intellectual is normally better off than they and can therefore avoid more easily the difficulties and hardships of life. Take, for example, a mother of seven who must work hard to bring up her family. I am less worried that she might miss the true meaning of Christianity than I am in my own case.

If we remain mere amateurs in the actual Christian life, if we have not in some way accepted to obey a law within the context of Christian freedom and self-restraint, then we are no more than miserable bunglers even if we do not carry too much real ballast of historical piety.

The Obligation through the Personal Call Over and
Above the Law

On the other hand, however, it must be said that just
because of its special character spirituality must be left
much freedom to realize itself in an individual way which
cannot be commanded and institutionalized. This goes
without saying because there is a true individual ethics;
this means that the adequate and total call the individual
receives from God does not only consist in the sum of the
general Christian moral and religious norms. We may even
say that spirituality begins only when all this has been fulfilled. Certainly the new element cannot simply be separated from one's ordinary life, but by fulfilling the precepts
of the catechism and the commandments of the Church
and being in this sense a good Christian, we have not yet
adequately responded to God's call to our concrete and
unique person. There are Christians who are aware of
God's call in the choice of their profession, their marriage
partner and similar decisions—but they are few. This is
not meant to advocate an integralism of piety according
to which one is a good Christian only if all one's actions
are reflected and integrated into theoretical norms; it does
not mean that all realized freedom must be passed as it
were through the filter of reflection in order to be responsible action. This is certainly not the case. Nevertheless,
there is an individual ethics, that is a completely personal
and unique responsibility for our life, the direction it takes
and even more so for what we do in it. The good Samaritan
who cared for the man who had fallen among the robbers
did not say: let the police do that, or, let the priest take
care of him, for he has more time than I, and if they don't
do it, why should I? But it is precisely I who may not run
away from this obligation, which is part of my life. Per-

haps the priest has passed him by for a very good reason; perhaps it was high time for him to take a service, and he could not keep his congregation waiting, for that was more important! Perhaps he escaped damnation because of his stupidity or his narrow religious outlook; but the other man had to pick up the wounded man. Thus there are innumerable things in life which are asked from *me* and from nobody else, so that I cannot hide behind an anonymous crowd, public opinion or other obligations. From this individual ethics which has nothing to do with a wrongly understood situation ethics personal piety receives a character which far surpasses the generally necessary legal aspect of spirituality.

Seeking New Forms of Spirituality

We are today in a very difficult transition period with regard to earlier forms and ideals of spirituality. How can we still be genuinely devout without practising a stale piety that is no longer relevant to modern life, how can we do more than live on the periphery of the Church? How can one combine being a reasonable and lively, I won't even say a happy human being with being a genuinely pious Christian in such a way that both are at least approximately one? For we cannot ask for more than that, since everybody lives somehow in a pluralistic way. For in this transition period, when Christianity and the Church must adapt themselves to quite a new way of life, theologians can only make very abstract suggestions. Thus the contemporary Christian, especially the intellectual and even more the theologian, has the duty to seek and find anew the patterns for the spiritual life of today and tomorrow. Neither Pope nor bishop nor priest can dispense him of this duty which may cost him immense effort and sacrifice.

This does not, of course, mean simply abandoning the old formulae which are rightly or often also wrongly declared obsolete, and just living irresponsibly from day to day. We may, for example, say theoretically: There must certainly be something like "meditation" in the life of the genuine Christian; but it is not so simple to say what this means in practice, and I would not presume to proffer effective recipes. Men are different; traditions which are still alive in one place may be impossible to preserve in another, etc. But no one can pretend to neglect the question altogether because at the moment no reasonable solutions have emerged. I cannot say, for example, whether the pilgrimage of the French students from Paris to Chartres corresponds to the mentality of modern man. There are so many things in Christian devotion including the liturgy and its paraliturgical elements which still exist, and with which one may not experiment merely because the traditional forms of worship wrongly seem to be boring. Of course, there must be experiments, but they must contain the elements of a certain progress. A teacher of religion, for example, must foster in the young people the central Christian experience; hence he ought to be able to help them through his own religious practice without asking them to invent anew everything belonging to the Christian life, which leads to nothing anyhow in ninety-five per cent of the cases.

Self-Criticism as Regulating the Claim to Freedom

One should not be called "conservative" in the bad sense if one also speaks of the limits of freedom in this connection. In my opinion the best proof of an authentic synthesis between Christian freedom and a serious affirmation also of an external law is a critical attitude to oneself. There are enough reasons for criticizing existing customs, and this criticism is also to be expressed. But it is strange how convinced we are that our own opinion must be right though we admit theoretically that others are on the average not much more stupid than we are and also by and large want to do the right thing. But in practice we often forget this simple fact which no reasonable person will deny, if we claim complete freedom for ourselves, whereas the love of peace and unity should make us more cautious and humble. St. Paul's Letter to the Romans has some very relevant things to say on this subject.

Fundamentally we may say this: there is no law against the man who truly has faith, hope and love and who genuinely loves his neighbour and can surrender himself. In this love, it seems to me, law and freedom merge into the freedom of God's grace.

The Prayer of the Individual and the Liturgy of the Church

So far the Second Vatican Council has been the only Ecumenical Council to discuss the liturgy. In the history of the liturgy and the liturgical movement this is certainly a highwater mark that can hardly be surpassed. The principles of the liturgy are no longer merely lived; they are reflected in theology and liturgical law. So it looks at least as if these principles could, indeed, still be applied in a practice which corresponds to the changing historical situation, but that they could no more be essentially surpassed. This is an event within the Church which has certainly not yet been sufficiently considered.

But this highwater mark occurred in a historical situation which invited the anxious question whether we were not at the peak of a historical process which could only be followed by a decline. For the triumph of the liturgy at Vatican II took place just when the question arose whether man was still capable of worship and liturgy, whether the "demythologization" of Christianity ought not to be accompanied by a "desacralization", and whether Christianity ought not to cease to be a religion at all. At the very time of its triumph the liturgy has been most radically called in question. At times it may even seem as if the official sanction of a greater liturgical freedom and renewal is already being used to bring about an almost suicidal desacralization. Thus we may finally be left with a liturgy which expresses only secularized human inter-relationships until these, too, have become superfluous. This is the strange situation in which the liturgy celebrates its triumph in the Church of the Second Vatican Council: while proclaiming itself officially as the centre of the Church it is at the same time profoundly threatened.

This, of course, is only one element of a greater and more comprehensive danger, which is the danger of losing the personal relation to God in prayer altogether. Indeed we may say, perhaps a little exaggeratedly but not without reason, the liturgy such as it is actually performed today—though, we hope, against its own ultimate principles—this liturgy itself increases this greater danger, because it often has a harmful influence on the private prayer of indi-viduals and groups. This may be disputed with regard to the principles of an authentic theology of the liturgy, but hardly as regards everyday practice.

There is, however, also a theoretical problem. For ever since Pius XII's *Mediator Dei* and also at the Second Vatican Council the liturgical prayer has been given such priority over the private prayer of individuals and groups that—despite papal warnings—one is easily tempted to think that private prayer is more or less superfluous, especially if we are as involved in our liturgical prayer as we ought to be. Here we should like to discuss this mis-understanding of the official declarations about such a preference for liturgical prayer, even though we cannot exhaust the subject. But the following observations may, perhaps, be of some little use to diminish a "liturgical triumphalism" which does not seem at all fitting in the present spiritual situation.[1]

---

[1] The author is here taking up a theme he has already treated in a more scholastic manner in the essay "Some Theses on Prayer 'in the

When speaking about the relation between liturgical und "private" prayer we should not forget that there is also a private prayer of groups (for example a family rosary or a devotion approved by the bishop) which may itself approach in various degrees to liturgical prayer, even to being virtually identical with it, so that there is only a verbal difference between the two. But here we will not discuss such differences or agreements.

I

First of all it must be said that according to the explicit teaching of the Church which is also expressed by Vatican II:[2]

a) There is a prayer of individuals and groups which is not liturgical prayer in the strict sense of the word.

b) The Sacred Liturgy has in a certain sense a higher dignity than the non-liturgical "pious exercises".

c) The higher dignity of liturgical prayer does not abolish the necessity and duty of private non-liturgical prayer. Such non-liturgical prayers are highly recommended if they conform to the spirit and law of the Church and especially if they are according to the mandate of the Apostolic See.

We shall not prove these statements by earlier doctrinal pronouncements, but confine ourselves to the teaching of Vatican II. Without producing an exact definition of the concept of liturgy this is contained especially in articles

Name of the Church'", *Theological Investigations*, V (1966), pp. 419–38. See this essay for particular details connected with this problem.

[2] For previous statements of the magisterium see *ibid.*, footnotes 10 (with further literature), 12 and 13.

12–13 of the Constitution on the Sacred Liturgy, which clearly express the three principles given above (on the third cf. also the final sentence of art. 7). Here a distinction is made between the *vita spiritualis* and the *Liturgiae participatio* as one of its parts. According to the whole context of arts. 12–13 the *pia populi christiani exercitia,* together with the episcopally approved devotions *(sacra Ecclesiarum particularium exercitia)* belong to this "spiritual life". The family prayer named in the Decree on the Apostolate of the Laity (art. 11) should also be mentioned in this context. Of all these pious exercises it is said, however, that they are far surpassed by the actual liturgy *(longe antecellere)* by virtue of its nature.[3]

II

These declarations of the magisterium do not solve, but rather pose the problem of the nature of non-liturgical common prayer and its relation to liturgical prayer proper, and this for many reasons of which only one will here be discussed more extensively.

[3] For the texts quoted see, for example, J. A. Jungmann's commentary on the Constitution on the Sacred Liturgy in H. Vorgrimler, ed., *Commentary on the Documents of Vatican II,* vol. I (1967), pp. 16–17. The commentary indicates that the Constitution on the Liturgy has not clarified certain important points. No unambiguous definition of "liturgy" has been attempted, and because of this it is not clear why episcopally instituted and controlled devotions (or, for example, the rite of the Corpus Christi procession) are not to be regarded as liturgy, as this text presupposes rather than teaches or states explicitly. Therefore the boundary between liturgy and private communal prayer is not very clear either, since this, where commended and directed, makes a fluid transition into episcopally controlled devotion. But we shall take the clause formulated under a) above as given, and shall inquire only as to its more precise meaning and its (limited) religious consequences.

We are not going to describe and discuss the concept of liturgy in the documents of Vatican II. For it is not so simple as it may appear to some, and the problem has actually not been unanimously solved by theologians. At the Council no actual definition of the liturgy has been worked out; this task was left to the theologians. For between the worship of the official Church which must certainly be called liturgy (the celebration of the Eucharist) and the private prayer of the individual which can certainly not be called liturgy, there is a no-man's land of transitional forms; and thus every definition of liturgical prayer depends to some extent on an arbitrary terminology rather than on the thing itself.

Hence, if it is said that "*the* liturgy far surpasses all other acts of piety", it is not at all clear whether this applies for certain to each individual pious exercise that is supposed to belong to the liturgy (for example a way of the cross made in common within a religious community). But, according to the declarations of the magisterium, the expression *longe antecellere* certainly applies only to the liturgy as a whole (i.e. together with the celebration of the Eucharist), not to any individual liturgical exercise as opposed to any non-liturgical prayer. We will here not discuss in detail in what sense and with what reservations the liturgy is to be called the first and necessary source of the Christian life and spirit (Decree on Priestly Formation, *Optatam Totius*, art. 16 Decree on the Appropriate Renewal of the Religious Life, *Perfectae Caritatis*, art. 6), of grace (Constitution on the Liturgy, art. 10) and the summit to which all the action of the Church is directed (*ibid.*, art. 10), and how all other Christian activity and prayer has its origin and goal in the liturgy. Such statements have to be interpreted with a certain discretion. For despite the interconnection of all the elements we must distinguish between the one saving act of Christ which is made present in the liturgy (though its efficacy is not restricted to this presence) and the external sacramental action as such. The statement on the central importance of the liturgy cannot be equally applied to both elements in isolation from each other. If it is primarily applied to the first element, it is a positive, but not an exclusive statement, since the saving power and importance of the redemptive work of Christ (as the worship of God and the sanctification of man) affect man not *only* through their cultic presentation in the liturgy. For it cannot, for example, be gainsaid that according to the whole Christian tradition martyrdom is the highest form of sharing in the Passion of Christ, that it cannot be surpassed by any other event in the Christian life and that it is the highest self-realization of the Church. For the Eucharist (like martyrdom!) makes present the unique paschal mystery of Christ; but it adds something to it only insofar as it is the act of the Church, hence existentially, in faith, hope and love, the act of those who celebrate the liturgy themselves. But this act is at least as much present in martyrdom, even more so than in the Eucharist, because it is "guaranteed" to be actually there. For it can surely not be seriously denied that, according to Mt 25, a man may encounter Christ in his neighbour more truly and decisively as his Saviour than in a eucharistic communion which, despite the Real Presence and its sacramental efficacy *ex opere operato* is but the sign and the means of that union with Christ in the Holy Spirit which happens in the difficulties of our daily life even unto our "dying in the Lord".

Here we cannot pursue these and other far-reaching considerations. We shall limit ourselves to a theological discussion of the declaration of the Second Vatican Council

(cf. also Pius XII's *Mediator Dei*) according to which the
liturgy "far surpasses" all private prayer. One of the
reasons for this preference is evidently the fact that the
liturgy is performed "in the name of the Church" (cf.
art. 98) while this cannot be said of private prayer. This
seems to me the point at which private prayer is most
threatened by an all too easy misunderstanding of the
present teaching on the liturgy. In our discussion we shall
ask first what theological statements can be made on the
subject of private prayer, examining afterwards if liturgical *prayer* (as distinct from the Eucharist and the administration of the sacraments with which we are not here
concerned) can be preferred to it at all, and if so, what
such a preference means for the practice of the Christian
life.

For the private prayer of the Christian, whether of the
individual or of a group, is no merely "private" affair
with which the Church has nothing to do. For such prayer,
too, is the prayer of those who have been justified and are
filled with God's grace. This prayer, too, is made in the
Holy Spirit who assists our weakness and says Abba—
Father with us. This prayer, too, is prayer of the baptized
who are fortified by the Spirit, of men and women filled
with grace and incorporated in the mystical Body of
Christ. For the spirit of Christ is the ground of prayer,
and all love of one's neighbour is related to God and Jesus
Christ, hence where two or three are gathered together in
his name (Mt 18:20) the Lord is in the midst of them.
Now, as the Holy Spirit is the ground of prayer, and as
every Christian is sacramentally and socially destined to
the worship of God by baptism and confirmation, therefore every justified person has an essential relation to the
Church, hence the Christian's private prayer, too, especially when it is made in common, has an inner relation to

this Church. It is an act of the Church in a true sense, even if not expressly commissioned by the authorities of the Church.

It would be wrong to assume that an act of the Church can be performed only on the basis of an "official" commission by the authority of the Church beyond that of baptism. For if this were the case, the sanctity and fruitful use of the grace that is given to individual Christians could not be attributed to the Church herself. But this is definitely done (cf. *D* 1794). The Church herself is *sancta Ecclesia* not only because of the objective holiness of her members. The act of the magisterium is not the same as the act of the Church, but the act of the magisterium is a certain species of the acts which are performed by the individual members of the Church and constitute the action of the Church in a true sense. If it can be said that the Church is a sinful Church because of the sins of her members (cf. Decree on Ecumenism, arts. 3 and 4), even though this sin contradicts her own nature and spirit, then we must attribute ecclesial importance even more to the good, inspired acts, hence also to all the prayers, of her members. If there is a "treasury of the Church" *(D* 550–2, 757, 1541; Paul VI, *Indulgentiarum Doctrina)* which consists actually in the active union with God of all justified Christians, then this, too, makes it clear that all acts of those justified in the Holy Spirit constitute the very life of the Church, hence that the action of the Church is not the same as the action of her official representatives or what is done explicitly in their name. This is implied also in the promise of Jesus (Mt 18:20); for how could an ecclesial character be denied to a group in whose midst is the Lord? If such a group is truly gathered together in the name of Jesus it represents the Church, especially if it prays in a way expressly recommended by the hierarchy.

But what, then, does it mean that the liturgical prayer far surpasses the private (even the common) prayer of Catholic Christians, as the Constitution on the Liturgy says (art. 12), repeating declarations of Pius XII? Why is it privileged?

Perhaps we may first mention that normally, if somebody praises or recommends something, he does not at the same time think of something else that might also deserve special mention. Indeed, he may easily use a one-sided and emphatic expression which ought not to be over-estimated. This must certainly be kept in mind when evaluating the *longe antecellere* of the Constitution on the Liturgy. A telling instance of such an exaggeration is Pius XI's statement that devotion to the Sacred Heart is *summa totius religionis,* the sum of all religion. One can certainly make sense of this, but it must also be said that what makes this devotion the sum of all religion is the whole of Christianity, which is indeed present in it, but not only in it, and thus the statement may be considered to be true. Nevertheless, what distinguishes it from other forms of Christian devotion is not that it is the sum of all religion, hence it may be misunderstood by less cautious readers. The same is true of the assertion that the liturgy is the source and goal of Christianity. This sentence is true in one sense, for the centre and origin of Christianity, God's gracious self-communication in the crucified and risen Christ, is indeed present in the liturgy. But taken in an exclusive sense the statement would be false; for this self-communication does not take place only in the sacraments and the liturgy. But the *longe antecellere* refers only to this and is therefore justified in a certain sense, but not absolutely.

Nor should we forget a modern trend which has already been mentioned. There is nowadays, among both Protestant and Catholic theologians, a fairly strong tendency fowards "desacralization", which means in the last analysis reducing the Christian life to mere secular neighbourliness. This tendency is wrong, for the worship of God in spirit and in truth has its place at the very centre of the Christian existence; hence it is all the more important not to aggravate this tendency unwittingly by emphasizing the narrowly cultic and liturgical elements in the Christian life to such an extent that the cry for desacralization becomes the inevitable extreme reaction against it. Where this tendency claims support from the New Testament this is justified only in so far as the difference between the cultic worship of God in a temple as a "sacred" place, at sacred times, through sacred persons as distinct from a profane, "unholy" people, and the adoration of God in spirit and in truth is not, indeed abolished, but radically relativized. There is also something else. Modern ecclesiology, sanctioned by Vatican II, does not start its description of the nature of the Church, like Bellarmin, with its social organization, but with the people of God, the mystical Body of Christ, primarily constituted by the unity of the justified in the Holy Spirit, the community of the redeemed, as distinct from their organization in a "society". Only from there does this ecclesiology arrive at the social organization of this holy community of the people of God, an organization which is certainly necessary and conforming to the will of Christ, but nevertheless secondary. Thus it becomes clear that the liturgy of this Church does not only consist in the external ceremonial, but that it must be credited also with all the interior grace and glory that belongs to a Church which is more than a mere legal organization. On the other hand, however, it also becomes evident that the official order of prayer of the Church as a society must also be the prayer of the

Church as the people of God in the Holy Spirit. In other words, liturgical prayer is based on the spiritual power of prayer inherent in the people of God as the body of Christ. A liturgical order of prayer exists because prayer as such exists, the former does not create the latter, but on the contrary presupposes it, in the same way as sacraments exist only because there is grace which precedes both ontologically and historically its social (though efficacious) expression in the sacraments. We do not deny that liturgical and private prayer depend on one another, but because of the very nature of the Church it must be said that private prayer, especially if made in common, has a priority over official liturgical prayer whose ground and centre it remains. All this must not be forgotten if the *longe antecellere* of the Constitution on the Liturgy is to be rightly understood.

Now what is the advantage of liturgical over private prayer, if this advantage is reduced to its proper proportion?

We would stress again that, in order to keep the question within manageable limits, we here compare only liturgical and private prayer, hence leave aside the Eucharist as sacrifice and sacrament as well as the sacraments in general. To say it quite simply: the advantage of liturgical over private prayer is small. For the true dignity of Christian prayer is common to both and cannot be surpassed: both are the prayer of the holy people of God, both take place within the Body of Christ and in his presence, both are supported by the Holy Spirit. The nature and general dignity of all prayer are not enhanced by the official authorization of the Church, at least not through the addition of another, superior value. Such an authorization only includes this prayer in the social and official dimension of the Church, thus regulating it and giving it a certain guar-

antee that it actually corresponds to its own nature and to
that of the Church and encouraging a certain frequency
and regularity. Thus no values are attributed to liturgical
prayer which, by themselves and *in abstracto,* might not
also be conceded to private prayer. It is useful and valuable, but mainly as a service, and this is subordinate to the
real essence of all (common) prayer. This applies especially
to those "private" prayers which are nevertheless recommended and regulated by the Church such as the rosary,
approved litanies, prayers enriched with indulgences, episcopally approved devotions and so forth. It also applies
particularly to "private" prayer made in common. Members of the Church are always authorized to do this, even
sacramentally through baptism and confirmation. Wherever a baptized Christian in the state of grace approaches
God in prayer, also when praying to the Father in heaven
in his secret chamber or in "the domestic sanctuary of the
Church" (Decree on the Apostolate of the Laity, art. 11)
together with other members of his family, he prays as a
member of the Body of Christ, living its life, receiving
from it and giving to it.

Hence non-liturgical prayer may well in certain cases
be holier and of greater value for the Church than liturgical prayer. This indisputable fact should not be too easily
passed over with the famous scholastic distinction that
this happens *per accidens* (accidentally). For this "accident" is ordered by God who does, indeed, partly involve
us in the institutional Church and her worship, but not
altogether. For he gives his grace according to his good
pleasure, both in the liturgy and outside it, and hence
allows us to experience it where it is most easily and
authentically accessible. Who would deny, for example,
that the prayer of a martyr in his lonely prison cell before
his execution, in which he unites himself completely with

the death of Christ has greater dignity and validity before God and for his Church than many liturgical prayers? As long as a person preserves his external union with the Church by fulfilling his duties, he may well himself decide in Christian freedom whether he prays better, that is to say with greater faith, hope and love at home or at a liturgical celebration. The practice of the religious Orders and Congregations, too, shows that the freedom of the children of God obtains in this sphere. For there are those that have hardly any liturgical community prayers apart from the common celebration of the Eucharist, while otherwise everyone prays by himself. Moreover, if the Constitution on the Liturgy emphasizes that we ought to "pray without ceasing", this can hardly apply only to liturgical prayer, especially in the case of the laity, who would not have sufficient time for this; and so it may be concluded that in our daily life private and liturgical prayer need certainly not compete with each other.

Of course, the real threat to personal "private" prayer does not come from the liturgy, even though an indiscreet and ultimately untheological recommendation of liturgical prayer is an additional danger. The real danger affecting both liturgical and private prayer is the apparent or real lack of religious experience, of the courageous belief that we may prayerfully invoke the profound mystery of our existence and in doing so not only project ourselves and our needs. This would involve the special question of the meaning and possibility of the prayer of petition. All this cannot be discussed here. We can only say once more that liturgical prayer must not be understood in such a way as to prejudice private prayer, because in this case liturgical prayer, too, would be threatened.

Democracy in the Church?

The question mark in the title ought really to follow each of the nouns. For this heading does not only pose the difficult question whether democracy is possible and desirable or perhaps in a certain measure even present in the Church, but also raises that other problem of what democracy is in itself, without reference to the Church, and what makes it desirable. It goes without saying that we cannot answer this second question here, though we are well aware of the fact that the problem of democracy in the Church depends in large measure on the answer which we cannot provide to this other question. Hence our discussion will necessarily suffer from this defect. The difficulties of all countries on both sides of the Iron Curtain show that democracy in its proper sense is not guaranteed simply by the general suffrage of a so-called representative democracy. Much that is anything but true democracy may hide behind the façade of representative democracy; on the other hand, a society which is not democratically constituted in the normal sense of the word may sometimes achieve what a democracy aims at. But, as has been said, lack of space forbids a discussion of the essence of democracy, its possibilities and its dangers. We only presuppose it to be that form of society which grants its members the greatest possible freedom and participation in its life and decisions, in accordance with their intellectual, cultural and social condition.

I shall first discuss some principles concerning the question: Democracy in the Church? In a longer second section something will then be said on the concrete possibilities of a greater democratization of the Roman Catholic Church in accordance with her own doctrines.

A

In the first section three points will be discussed: First, the basic relationship between democracy and the Church, secondly a fundamental difference between applying the concept of democracy to secular society and applying it to the Church, and thirdly that despite this radical difference the question about democracy in the Church may yet be posed.

I

There is an inner basic relationship between what is meant or realized by democracy and the Catholic Church. This results from the fact that the Church is a community of those who freely believe and freely unite for the profession of faith and for worship. Taken as a society, the Church is based purely on the free faith of her members. Certainly, similar to secular society the Church, too, rests on certain presuppositions which are not produced by the free decision of her members and their free association as such, but are the very conditions of her existence, namely human nature, the saving will of God, redemption through Jesus Christ, the general call of all men to the Church and the resulting "duty" to belong to her. But all this does not alter the fact that the responsible adult (leaving out of

account infant baptism and its consequences) belongs to
the Church only by his free decision and that she can claim
him only on this condition. Members of a secular society
may belong to it through compulsion, and then the question arises how they may be guaranteed as large a sphere
of freedom and as free and active a cooperation as possible.
Thus in the state all democratic elements are meant to
counteract compulsory membership, while in the Church
free association is not only an end but actually a presupposition. Hence the ultimate meaning and end of all democracy is the very precondition of the Church. This, of
course, does not mean that there is, avoidably as well as
unavoidably, much that is "undemocratic" in the Church,
if for no other reason than that the baptized children must
slowly be led by the Church to a free and responsible
decision of personal faith without which no adult can be
a member of the Church in the fullest sense. Nevertheless,
there is a basic difference between the state which presupposes and practises compulsory membership and the
Church, in which the membership of responsible adults is
constituted only by the free act of faith. This alone is an
element of freedom and democracy in the fundamental
essence of the Church which does not, indeed, render the
question of democracy in the Church superfluous, but
which makes it much less vital, as is also the case in other
free associations.

The inner relationship between democracy (or that
which it is meant to guarantee) and the Church is ev-
idenced also by the essential charismatic element in the
nature of the Church. For all democratic institutions in a
state are meant to secure the necessary freedom for individuals and groups to produce free initiatives and decisions outside the sphere of social manipulation and planning. In the Church the charismatic elements correspond

to these unplanned activities for which a democratic constitution must leave room. True, the constitution of the
Church does not provide an absolute guarantee that these
charismatic elements which are given her by the freely
acting Spirit of God are always accorded the necessary
freedom for their development. In individual cases the
exact opposite may happen: the institution may hinder
and suppress the charismatic elements, in the words of
Scripture, it may extinguish the spirit. Nevertheless, two
points must be made:

First, the Church acknowledges this charismatic element
as an essential factor of her own nature. She does not mean
to be a totalitarian religious society whose life and decisions are all ruled by the orders of a central authority.
However much the Church may emphasize institution and
authority, she does not want at all to be an authoritarian
or totalitarian system. Hierarchy and institution are only
part of the Church, not ultimate and essential constituents
destined to manipulate her history and spirit in totalitarian
fashion. For the ministry of the Church is from the very
beginning a service of the free charisma, of the discernment
of spirits, a service of the unity and loving community of
the many charisms which the one autonomous Spirit of
God gives to his Church. A democracy may take many
constitutional forms; perhaps it may best be defined negatively as a people's constitution by which any totalitarian
manipulation of men is rejected and prevented. In this
fundamental sense the Church may be called a democracy
because she definitely recognizes the free charismatic
element that cannot be institutionalized as one of her
essential traits.

Secondly, if we believe in God's eschatological promise
to the Church of Christ we must be convinced that his
Spirit will preserve the institutional Church both at the

decisive moment and indefinitely from suppressing or manipulating its charismatic elements. True, such belief can also be a dangerous temptation not to take totalitarian tendencies in the Church sufficiently seriously. Nevertheless it is justified and contains the hope that the very danger inherent in this belief will not become overwhelming. Despite bitter individual disappointments this faith has not been fundamentally denied, for the free charismatic elements in the Church always find an outlet and make use also of her institutional factors. These charisms may well be called the democratic aspects of the Church, especially as it is evident from dogmatic ecclesiology as well as from church history that this freely working Spirit can be active not only in the official ministry of the Church but also in every individual of the *demos,* that is to say of the people of God. A relationship between democracy properly understood and the Church can also be deduced from a feature of the Church which at first sight would seem to be undemocratic. By divine and therefore immutable right the Church has a ministry that is represented by individual persons. This must be realized despite all collegial structures formed by the unity of the collegial presbyterium with its diocesan bishop. There are certain functions in the Church, for example the primatial powers of a local bishop, which must be performed by the individual and cannot be delegated to a group, so that the individual minister would only execute the latter's decision.

At first glance this characteristic of the Catholic Church may seem very undemocratic. But it is actually a guarantee of true democracy not only in name but in fact. For such personalism (if it may be so called) does not exclude a "democratic" election of these ministers and does not, in principle, prejudice a cooperation in their decisions by the

whole people of God or individual groups. On the other
hand such personalism *iuris divini*, which despite its importance cannot here be proved theologically, is a principle
of resistance against the well-known dangers and short-
comings of democracy in large societies where self-govern-
ment by the people, for example, by plebiscite is no longer
possible and the representation which takes its place becomes more and more autonomous. In such democracies
there is a real danger that no one knows any more who
makes the decision and is ultimately responsible for it,
hence to whom the member of such a society must apply
to make his views effectively heard. In a society, however,
in which the individual official cannot hide behind an
anonymous institution, but where one can appeal to an
individual conscience, to a person who is ultimately
responsible, where one can still distinguish between cause
and effect, basic reason and mere symptom, in such a
society the true purpose of democracy is fulfilled. For
democracy wants all the members of a society to cooperate
freely in its activities and decisions, and this is easier in
a society such as has just been described than in one where
the individual no longer knows where responsibility lies
and feels himself merely as a cog in a machine.

II

Having thus discussed a basic relationship between democracy and the Church, we must now draw attention to a
fundamental difference between democracy in the Church
and in a secular society.

This difference forbids us simply to apply all the democratic patterns and demands of a secular society to the
Church. For according to Catholic ecclesiology the fundamental constitution of the Church is of divine right and

hence immutable. This principle is valid even though in the beginning this constitution was only "lived" unreflectingly. It began to develop in apostolic times and entered the Church's consciousness only slowly in the process of doctrinal development. This is evident from the fact that even today the Church has no written constitution such as most modern states possess. The Church has an immutable basic constitution given in the divine revelation of Jesus Christ, and this is not subject to the will of the people. Now it might be said that insofar as the modern constitution of a state claims the respect of the citizens, it also presupposes certain fundamental human rights, the principles of the natural law and so forth, hence that it, too, has a basis which does not depend on the will of the citizens. Thus the relation between a democratic constitution and the preconditions of its positive law would be analogous to that between the human and variable canon law and the divine structures of the Church.

But this analogy ought not to obscure the essential difference between the constitution of the Church and that of the state. In the Church certain very concrete constitutional structures which might very well be different are of divine right, and this is not so in secular societies. Secular society gives itself its constitution, while this is not the case in the Church. For the constitution of the Church has been given to her by God in Jesus Christ, including also elements that belong to historical conditions. It may be asked whether such elements of divine right which derive from the revelation in Jesus Christ can be called "constitution" in the modern sense of the word, or whether this term should be applied only to the whole amalgam of divine and human right which forms the constitution of the Church. This is an interesting and not unimportant question, but it is after all only concerned with terminology and hence irrelevant in this context. For it does not change the fundamental fact that not everything in the Roman-Catholic Church is left to the democratic will of the Christian people, including its ministers.

This limits the question of democracy in the Church at least in a formal sense. For in a material sense nothing has yet been decided negatively about a democratic structure of the Church, just as little as in the case of a secular constitution which forbids the destruction of the democratic system and thus limits the possible will of the citizens. In practice, however, this means that the primacy of the Pope, for example, defined by the First Vatican Council, is not, in its truly democratic nature (which does not mean in a certain historical form!) subject to the will of the people or even of the college of bishops if this should differ from the will of the Pope and would want to change the constitution.

This leads us to another aspect which shows the fundamental difference between democracy in the Church and democracy in a secular society. We have already mentioned that in the Church, unlike in secular society, there exists no compulsory membership of responsible adults, and that this is, indeed, impossible because it would contradict the nature of the Church as a community of a faith of whose very essence it is that it must be free. This implies that a man who definitely contradicts the dogmatic faith of the Church can no longer be her member in the full sense of the word. If any members of the Church including also individual bishops were to demand that the Church should alter her constitution in a way contradicting her dogmatically defined self-understanding, such movement in favour of change would actually no longer take place within the Church but outside, for those demanding such a change could no longer belong to the Church in the full sense of a visible society. True, such demands are sometimes made by Catholics, who nevertheless do not want to leave the Church and may continue to take an active part in her life. But this changes nothing in the Church's own understanding of her given basic constitution which limits certain democratic tendencies.

It might, of course, be asked what would happen if a large majority of Catholics, possibly supported by some bishops, would nevertheless begin to dispute the Church's own conception of herself and attempt to remove hitherto dogmatically compulsory structures, as has actually happened earlier in the history of the Church. We can only answer that such an attempt at a "democratic" revolution from below against the dogmatic, and not only the canonically binding constitution of the Church will always remain a danger.

Hence it must be emphasized that the Roman Catholic Church exists only where her irreversible (even though historically developing) dogmatic conception is preserved. It is part of the hope of the Christian faith that there will always be a believing people, though not necessarily increasing in number, and that the Church as the sacrament of the salvation of the world will continue in existence. According to this indestructible hope the Spirit of the Church will always provide sufficiently for a faithful people as his body and thus prevent a revolution against the constitution of the Church that would destroy her.

Another element of Catholic ecclesiology makes clear the fundamental difference between democracy in the Church and in secular society. We will not here discuss difficult questions of a Christian philosophy about society and state, especially not in how far a representative of power in the secular state receives his authority not simply from the electorate. In any case, it must be said that a minister of the Church does not receive his powers simply from the Church people whose will he executes, but that he preaches the gospel, administers the sacraments and shares in the government of the Church because he is sent by Christ. This is yet another difference between a secular democratic society and the Church, which prevents us from simply applying the pattern of the former to the Church. This different origin of the Church's authority does not, of course, exclude, but rather implies that her ministry is possible only within the sanctified people of the redeemed and that it does not confront them from outside. The fact that this authority comes from Christ in no way contradicts a democratic manner of appointing its ministers, nor does it contradict the fact that their decisions are determined by the nature of man as well as by the gospel in such a way that they are not without relation to the will of the Christian people.

III

Despite the difference between secular and ecclesial democracy the question of democracy in the Church is nevertheless very relevant. For grace and its historical appearance in the concrete Church contain what we call nature as an element within themselves. Now human nature demands democracy at least from a certain historical phase of man's development onwards, hence it cannot be a matter of indifference to the Church, which consists of persons making legitimate demands for freedom and active cooperation, at least in the present state of her development. The Church, being a community of faith, must always correspond to the actual state of man's historical development. Moreover, only very little in the constitution of the Church is really of immutable divine law, and this law itself will inevitably exist in concrete historical forms which are not simply unchangeable. The papal primacy, for example, is of divine right, but this does not mean that the legal and administrative forms in which this primacy appears today share in its permanence. If we really take seriously the genuine historicity of man and also of the Church we cannot even adequately distinguish between their essence and their historical and accidental manifestations. Nor can we predict under what forms this permanent nature will appear in the course of history. This is left to the future, so that democratic tendencies may well contribute to the changed appearance of a permanent being. Thus the question: Democracy in the Church? implies an evernew historical synthesis between the constant nature of the Church and her concrete historical appearance, between *ius divinum* and *ius humanum,* between human and divine characteristics. A Catholic Christian and theologian will know that there is not only a history of the consciousness of faith, but also a history of dogma, hence that he possesses what is permanent in his faith and his Church only in history and not outside it, and he will therefore have no reason to be afraid of a development of the Church's constitutional law. He can certainly not reject as illegitimate a dynamic of history originating in a democratic will which affect the future history of his Church.

B

In the second section of our considerations we should like to make several points explaining the possibility of a "democratic" development of the Church without, however, claiming completeness.

I

We are not concerned in this context with brotherliness, freedom, spiritual tolerance or the view of every ministry in the Church as a mere service of the people of God. All this is to be presupposed. But we want to discuss social structures and institutions which would enable the people of God that has come of age not only as citizens but as Christians to take an active part in the life and decisions of the Church.

Insofar as such structures and institutions are of legal character they may, of course, be regarded as merely human and thus mutable, not necessary laws, because they did not always exist but have been—or have still to be—established. Nevertheless it must also be emphasized that such law is not left to the arbitrary will of the authorities only because it exists by custom or by a legal act and is therefore of human, not divine right. The Christian people suspect, and not always without reason, that because the Church's human law must be established by the authorities it is actually subject to the arbitrariness of the ministry and hence not really a law that would give the people a well-established position over against the decisions of the Pope or the entire episcopate.

In principle this suspicious attitude to the human law of the Church is unjustified. In a certain historical situation even the so-called human law of the Church may be required by an absolute moral demand or even by *ius divinum*. At a certain moment of history a special temporary form of the permanent nature of the Church as the community of free faith, hope and love may, indeed, become absolutely essential. In fact innumerable legal statutes and decisions would have been possible in the abstract, yet were never realized because they were not in harmony with the concrete situation of Church people. On the other hand, many structures and institutions have continued even against a possible opposition by individual authorities, though they were only of human law. If, therefore, we discuss future human structures and institutions of the Church which would make possible a more active participation of the laity in the decisions of ecclesiastical authorities, such efforts should not be discredited in advance by saying that they would remain in any case subject to the good pleasure of the hierarchy. Not everything that is legally possible can also be realized in practice. The Church authorities are prevented from carrying out whatever is within their moral and legal competence by concrete situations and by the mentality of Catholics who will thus have more room for cooperation, even where this is not strictly defined. We will now suggest a few institutions and structures that may help to bring about a true democratization of the Church.

II

Some such structures and institutions are already in process of development, even though only tentatively and slowly. I am thinking of parish councils, lay advisory committees and similar institutions which aim at giving the laity greater responsibility and cooperation in the decision-making of the Church. It is essential that despite the special authority of the episcopal office, such lay organizations should be given a genuine right of participation, and also that they should be truly representative of the laity. Of course, such a legally guaranteed cooperation and truly representative selection of the laity will give rise to many problems which cannot be discussed here. For in the

Church many things have to be done differently from the way in which they are done in secular democratic societies. For it can hardly be imagined that in the Church parties will come between the lay committees and the individual Christians which will enable the latter to form an opinion on ecclesiastical matters and to select their representatives accordingly. But if this seems unsuitable in the case of the Church (though it might be given some thought), the election of lay representatives beyond the small groups of the parish is a difficult question, especially as the Catholic associations no longer have a function similar to that of the political parties in appointing such representative bodies. Appointment by higher authority is also ruled out, because it might prejudice true lay representation, and so it is not easy to say how such representative bodies should be formed on the diocesan and national levels. The method of forming the higher body from representatives of those immediately below it does not seem very suitable either. Thus there are still many unsolved questions in the matter of lay representation.

Then there is the fundamental problem how such a body of lay representatives can be formed and can act in such a way that it remains within the framework of the divine constitution of the Church and her dogma, while also developing its own initiative and a justified critical function with regard to ecclesiastical authority. True, the right relation between the hierarchical ministry and the laity can never be completely regulated by institutional and legal methods, but involves also an element of human freedom as well as of the spirit of the Church. Nevertheless, this should not prevent us from creating a sound dialogical relationship between hierarchy and laity also by giving the latter institutional rights. We have only made a beginning in solving these problems, and it needs courage and mutual confidence between hierarchy and laity if we are to make progress. If, on the contrary, both were to mistrust each other, each side regarding the other as hostile to its own rights, then the democratization of the Church through the creation of lay bodies could only result in strife and schism, or at most in a bureaucracy occupied only with itself. Both sides must have courage to practise Christian love and hope, they must be prepared to believe that each wants to help the other.

III

Another way of a possible democratization of the Church without prejudice to its divine constitution probably belongs to a rather distant future, if it should once more be realized at all. I mean something like an election of the ministers of the Church by the Christian people themselves. This is by no means incompatible with the basic constitution of the Church *iuris divini*. For this had been possible in the early Church and exists even today at least in very rudimentary form in the institution of the so-called patronates and in certain rights of the congregations in some Swiss cantons regarding the appointment of their parish priests. Hence an influence of the laity on the "designation" of ministers, for example of parish priests and bishops, is not in principle opposed to the constitution of the Church, because such cooperation does not prevent the authority of these ministers from being rooted in Christ and his always hierarchical Church, rather than in the accidental number of electors. Besides, for such election to be valid it must always take place in implied or express agreement with the entire ministry, represented by all the bishops under the Pope. On the other hand, these conditions do not exclude in principle a true election *iuris humani*, from below.

We would not, however, assert that a true "democratization" of the Church would exist automatically and certainly if parish priests or bishops were elected by the people, and this election could no longer be the sole right of the authorities. Leaving aside the fact that unsuitable ministers might also be elected democratically and that it is also possible for the people to influence the appointment of ministers without this being laid down by law, the question arises how this election is to be effected. The size of modern dioceses and probably also of most parishes makes an election by plebiscite almost impossible, especially as the majority of the people really cannot know whether a certain candidate possesses the necessary qualifications for his office. But if an election by plebiscite is ruled out, we are again faced with the question which body of electors would represent the actual people. This question leads to another, namely which among all those who give their religion as R. C. should cooperate in appointing the electoral bodies. For many nominal Catholics may not live a Christian life at all and may be quite uninterested in the Church, but might nevertheless claim their right to vote for electoral bodies precisely in order to work against the interests of the Church. Surely such Catholics ought not to have such a vote.

Thus it is understandable that the idea of giving the laity a say in the election of ministers is not meant for the near future. If, as seems probable, the Church becomes increasingly a community of committed Christians rather than a Church of the people, conditions will probably come into being which will make such an election easier, perhaps even natural.

IV

There is perhaps another possibility of a future genuine democratization of the Church. For she may recognize small groups of Christians which develop independently of the territorial principle as Christian communities with the same institutional stability and rights that have so far been accorded only to the parishes. For up to now the individual Christian has established a social relation with the Church more or less exclusively through the *territorial* parish, which is an administrative section of the diocese. But if the diaspora situation of the Church increases and becomes more obvious, it may become impossible to appoint a parish priest to every parish. In this case the Church may not only tolerate the free formation of Christian communities apart from the territorial principle, but may even consider it desirable. Such groups, created from below, may well gain proper institutional stability.

Now, if we be allowed an imaginative look into the future, such communities might in certain circumstances choose an "elder" (presbyter) from their midst who would then become their priestly president through sacramental ordination by the bishop. Such a priest would, of course, have to possess the necessary qualifications of a Christian way of life and theological knowledge, but he would not have to be seminary-educated. In such a community the democratization of the Church on this level would have solved itself.

This, too, is probably an image of future conditions which may not even be very happy, but which cannot be rejected as mere fantasy. The more deeply the Church enters into the diaspora situation, the more necessary such a future may become, in which the responsible cooperation of the whole laity which will then still exist becomes an

absolute necessity. Then many problems of the so-called
democratization of the Church will probably solve themselves, because then the laymen will no longer see the ministry only as a given entity but as something that he himself wills and that is supported by his own free obedience
of faith in the Church. Such a freely accepted authority
would no longer have problems of "democratization".

Such a development would cause the unfortunate antagonism between hierarchy and people to disappear and
to be replaced by a healthy polarity between the two. Such
a new relationship could be practised first and most easily
by those Christian communities which will probably come
into existence from below and will be authorized by the
hierarchy.

V

We should like to draw attention also to another aspect of
meaningful democratization of the Church. Pius XII had
already emphasized the necessity of a public opinion in the
Church. But this cannot exist if one conceives it as a unanimous applause for whatever the ecclesiastical authorities
decide or desire. Certainly, a public opinion in and of the
Church must remain within the framework of the one
compulsory profession of faith and also of a general
readiness to obey the authorities. This, however, does not
mean that there cannot be serious differences of theological opinion within the Church, nor that a Christian could
never refuse to obey a certain particular order of a minister
of the Church because his conscience considers it as incompatible with justice or charity, despite the minister's good
faith. We must get used to such disagreements within the
Church. We must learn that the unity of the faith and the

will to obedience and love are not abolished by certain tensions. Both sides must get used to this: the authorities which must not imagine that peace and quiet are the foremost necessity, and the laity who must not think that revolution and rebellion against authority and arbitrary theological opinions are ideal attitudes only because there may be theological differences and cases of disobedience.

Once a certain pluralism in the Church and in her public opinion has been understood and practised, a fair democratic attitude will become easier for both sides.

Theology's New Relation to the Church

Theology finds its own nature and becomes truly interesting only when it is not the personal theology of an individual theologian, but when it is "ecclesial" theology. For theology must always remain within the Church's reflection on the Word of God. I am, of course, well aware that there are many other and much more relevant subjects for a theologian than the relation of his work to the Church *(Kirchlichkeit)*, and that he can present himself only somewhat indirectly and perhaps not without misunderstandings in this way. Nevertheless, this subject makes sense. It is new probably only in this sense that today this problem has become more urgent, even though it has recurred again and again in Church history ever since gnosticism.

I will begin this theme with a very modest and subjective discussion. I presuppose, of course, that there is such a thing as theology and that it is meaningful. Whether theology can be called a science is of no fundamental importance; it depends on what one means by science, a question that cannot be answered by any single science. Hence we will here simply presuppose that theology in general and Christian theology in particular is possible and meaningful.

First of all, one's own opinion as distinct from that of others does not seem to be particularly important. I know, of course, that in trying to arrive at the subject itself, which is not simply the same as my opinion of it, I cannot bypass this opinion. For the subject concerned will always be part of my experience, from which I cannot escape and for which I am intellectually responsible to myself as well as to others, which only I can turn into the law of my life. Thus the subject itself cannot be found outside one's own opinion as such, because a person can never escape from himself; but this does not mean that what interests me in this opinion is the appearance of my own subjectivity. What draws my attention is the subject itself and the common traits which appear in it. Even subjectivity is interesting only insofar as it is also a medium or is silently received by the person as something objective and carried throughout his own history. To say it more simply and exactly, my starting point is always to consider myself in principle not more clever and more honest than others. True, in a particular case I do claim the right to be more objective, farseeing and wiser than a certain other person whose opinion I encounter, but I do this only because I attribute reason and honesty to all men, at least in principle, and hence also to myself, not because I prefer my own subjective opinions. I am convinced that I must always be very critical and distrustful of my own opinions, because it is more difficult to be objective about oneself than about others, and so the danger of deceiving oneself is greater than that of being deceived by the opinion of others.

Of course, such a position presupposes the conviction that the object and its communicability are not hopelessly denied us, and that if we can possess the common object at all, we can do so only subjectively.

But if we start with this position which appears whenever we begin to speak to each other, then it goes without saying that in principle the opinion of another must be as important to me as my own. Indeed, truth will become truly my own precisely when my subjectivity is living in constant mutual give and take with others and their truth. A truth which were exclusively my own would be the hell of absolute loneliness in which the subject would be condemned to nothing but its own society. The truth which the subject truly gives itself by freeing it from mere solipsistic subjectivity, this truth exists only in permanent dialogue. And this, again, can take place only if we trust that we do not simply and ultimately disagree but that we are seeking in common a truth which we already possess in common in our life, even if we do not yet know it in the notional reflection without which we could not speak to each other at all. A mysterious deeper unity is presupposed even by the most violent controversy, which we may not avoid merely for a quiet life. If such a unity did not exist a dialogue could not begin at all, because there would be no common ground between the partners from which to carry it on.

This applies generally to the truth which concerns man as such and hence transcends simple statements of particular facts which are the subject of the empirical sciences. This applies particularly to the ultimate truth which man wants to find or to receive, whether we call it the truth of religion or the truth of faith or anything else. In this sphere, which embraces everything else and cannot itself be again integrated into a higher order, truth can less than elsewhere be that merely subjective truth of a solipsistic individualism. *Weltanschauung*, to use such an inexact term, can least of all be some agglomeration of personal ideas. For it concerns man as a whole, and he exists only in genuine intercommunication with others. Man finds himself only by opening and entrusting himself to others and hence his self-interpretation which, if correct, is religion or at least some form of belief, can also happen only in the risk of this intercommunication. If a man wanted to have a completely private religion and had not yet succeeded in making others share his own opinion, this religion would necessarily be something quite arbitrary which should be uninteresting even to himself. But if this truth can only exist in open communication with others, it also necessarily involves what is good in others, however incapable of being assimilated this may appear at first sight. Nor should it be forgotten that if this intercommunication is accepted as it really is, it must necessarily include also an institutional and social element. For otherwise such intercommunication would finally remain in the purely private sphere, left to the good pleasure of the individual. Without any institutional factors the other person would exist for me only in so far as I permitted it, so that I would still regard him only as an element of my own subjectivity.

Where truth concerns the whole man it has necessarily to do with the institutional, as far as this, taken in a very wide sense of the word, represents that reality through which the other has a true importance for myself even before being accepted by the arbitrary decision of the individual. This truth makes demands on me though its institutional nature has not been decreed by me. But it can become my own solely if I not only tolerate it even though under protest, but also accept it and integrate it into my own freedom and decision. Nevertheless, the truth which must be whole and authentic for myself must also appear as that of the others, and it is truly free and not subject to being manipulated by my fancy only if it is institutional in the wider sense, so that it is actually, and not only ideally, independent of me. What has so far been said is no more than a certain formal and transcendental condition for the essential ecclesiality of theology. Its actual ecclesiality has not yet been reached, for this has, of course, other mate-

rial qualities which have to be more exactly brought out by
theology itself. To do this we should have to speak of the
"grace" of faith as the grace of the most radical intercommunication among men which is derived from God; we
should have to speak of the Christ event as God's escha-
tologically unsurpassable and victorious self-communication
to the world, and finally of the death and resurrection of
Christ; we should also have to say more exactly what is the
meaning of the Church as the community of those who
confess this eschatological historical appearance of God's
absolute self-communication to the world. But this we
cannot, of course, do here. We confine ourselves to the
starting point for an understanding of the ecclesiality of
theology such as has just been mentioned.

In our context this means that for the individual theologian there must be a concrete and independently acting
authority to which he accords a truly determining influence
on his theological thought and with which he carries on a
constant dialogue, so that his thought will not become a
mere monologue round his own ideas. For a Catholic it almost goes without saying that the written word of Scripture cannot be the partner in this dialogue. For a book must
be interpreted historically, and in our case also existentially. But both the course and the result of this interpretation presented to the reader will still be only the opinion
of the interpreter for which he will once more be held accountable by the book itself in an ideal, though certainly not
in a real sense. A book may become the occasion of a monologue, but not of a dialogue. It is read, but it does not speak
by itself. It may have an irreplaceable function in a dialogue, but it cannot carry it on. It can be an essential means
for the Church's part in the dialogue but it cannot be a
partner in it. If in this connection we would only refer to
the testimony of the Spirit who speaks in and through

Scripture, this would indeed be correct and would be acknowledged also in Catholic theology; but we would not yet have reached the question where the dialogue touches the human dimension as such. The active institutional side of this theological dialogue can certainly not replace the Spirit. But this Spirit, together with Scripture, can become an active opposing partner of one's own theological opinion only if he works in the institutional community which we call Church.

Nor does the discussion of theologians by itself constitute this authentic dialogical situation. It is, indeed, the forum of necessary controversy, of ever renewed doubting, of ever-new discussion of new situations within which the message of Christianity must be considered, but it is not the forum of decision, of the profession of faith rather than of theological questioning. Perhaps we ought here to express something more clearly that has so far remained implicit. For though theology as such may constantly discuss and question the confession of the Church, it remains nevertheless bound by it. Theology meditates on this confession, but it does not create it from the discussion which it represents. What theology always seeks it has always also already found; for the whole truth of man as opposed to partial questions and answers must always already be given if it is always to be questioned and found. For Christian theology this always given truth which theology questions and on which it reflects is present in the confession of the Church. In this dialogue of theology the institutional Church is the active and properly constituted partner. Her confession is not only question but also answer, so much so that the answer very often calls forth the question. In union with this confession the institutional Church becomes the active partner in her dialogue with the theologian, and this confession is situated in history, it is no rigid formula which can only be repeated monotonously. But where this confession is believed in with absolute conviction it cannot be revised but remains valid also for the future. Hence this confession with which the Church confronts the theologian must always be considered anew; it remains, and it changes in order to remain.

Basing ourselves on these brief and imperfectly described initial positions we would now say something more definite about the ecclesiality of Catholic theology such as it is seen by a contemporary theologian.

Catholic theology, too, is not only the repetition and scholastic analysis of what the magisterium of the institutional Church has proclaimed to be her confession, even though not all of it is equally binding. Theology has also a certain critical function with regard to the magisterium; it always questions what this teaching actually means. It confronts the doctrine of the Church with all the new questions and insights produced by the changing historical situation of the human spirit. Hence theology is an essential condition of the developing history of the Church's faith and creed. This is the case particularly as regards Catholic theology, since the Catholic faith implies the conviction of a plurality of human knowledge which is important also for this faith, a pluralism which is not simply administered by the Church. For secular knowledge may be of a kind either to make demands on the faith or to threaten it, though it is not within the competence of the Church's authority. In such cases theology has the duty to represent such knowledge to the Church and to enter into a dialogue with her. For theology speaks not only from but also to the Church; thus despite its essential ecclesiality which it can never give up without being annihilated, theology has a true dialogical relation to the Church and her confession.

If, therefore, a theologian is to do his duty, despite his

ecclesiality he will also be critical of the Church, he will produce creative controversy in order to reconcile what is as yet unreconciled. The theologian does not only represent the Church's confession before the world, he also represents the world and its constant movement of knowledge and action before the Church. Hence, precisely because he practises an ecclesial theology, he cannot always simply avoid conflicts with the Church's magisterium. He must want to be troublesome to the Church, because he represents that unrest and constant revolution by which the permanent confession of the Church always renews itself. This should really go without saying when the Church finds herself in a pluralism of knowledge which is religiously and philosophically relevant but not given by revelation, or, if we may call it thus, in a gnoseologically concupiscent situation, even though the nature of the conflicts possible in this situation cannot be exactly defined. Besides, it should be clear that a genuine conflict does not exist at all if there is an absolute rejection of the Church as a partner in a dialogue.

A more detailed discussion of this aspect of the theologian's dialogue with his Church cannot be attempted within the confines of this book. It goes without saying that such a conflict situation changes considerably according to the measure in which the faith itself is engaged in the ecclesiastical teaching with which the theologian is confronted. But according also to the Catholic understanding of theology, the theologian has sometimes the right and the duty to state his dissent from a teaching of the magisterium which does not absolutely engage the Church. In such a case he must present his view in a way that does justice to the ecclesial importance of his opinion, to the continuation of his dialogue with the magisterium und also to his respect for the latter's teaching. Here, of course, we cannot discuss all the rules given by fundamental theology for treating such discrepancies between theologians and magisterium. Such rules may, indeed, easily be accused of being merely legalistic. But if an opinion is admittedly important and the unity of a society unthinkable without truth and a binding ethos, such conflicts cannot be eliminated by declaring that the society is not concerned with an individual opinion at all. Or if this were done, one's own insight would be reduced to mere interiority and arbitrary fancy; thoughts would indeed be free, but in a sphere quite divorced from social reality. Hence in the Church as elsewhere we cannot do without rules which guide any conflict that has not yet been resolved in favour of one party in such a way that the dialogue between the opposing sides is not made impossible. In order to avoid misunderstandings it may be said in passing that such rules must be different in a society like the state of which one is a compulsory member, from those obtaining in a voluntary society like the Church, to which one need not belong. In the first case such rules must grant more freedom and take into account more violent conflicts while nevertheless supporting the dialogue, for the members of such a society are not free to leave it. In the second case, however, as for example in the Church, a person may retain the freedom of his conviction by leaving and by breaking off the dialogue within the Church.

Thus, despite the basic ecclesiality of theology there does exist a conflict-ridden dialogue between theologians and the institutional Church with her confession and her magisterium. But this dialogue can and should be sustained within the Church, and according to the Catholic faith it can remain in the Church. Nevertheless, it is possible that a theologian may be wrongly convinced that he contradicts absolutely a tenet definitely taught by the Church as absolutely binding, so that the dialogue becomes one that is carried on between the Church and an outsider, though he is officially still a member of the Church and does not want to leave her on his own account. Leaving aside this quite possible case, we may say that the dialogue between a theologian and the magisterium is an intra-ecclesial one, and the doctrine of this theologian an ecclesial doctrine only if he respects and accepts as binding that teaching which the Church considers inseparable from her faith and proclaims with absolute engagement. But a theologian may not accept this presupposition from the beginning, or he may try to eliminate it implicitly or explicitly by demanding that the Church should revise her faith or her idea of herself according to his theological opinion or that she should accept the latter as of equal right. In this case the dialogue between the Church and the theologian would—whether admittedly or not—have been replaced by a theological monologue in which the theologian produces and admits only his own opinion. The Church must be an authentic partner in a dialogue, independent of the opinion of an individual theologian; but this she can be only if she is not a formal and abstract entity capable of being changed by individual thought into just anything. I cannot talk seriously to an independent partner who would make absolutely everything a matter of choice and discussion, without any settled fundamental conviction whatsoever. In a certain sense all true discussion presupposes something that is indisputable even if this indisputable is itself discussed, as happens in metaphysics and theology. The extent of what is not open to discussion may vary considerably according to the different partners; it may, in certain cases, even be reduced to the conviction that men must talk to each other fairly and honestly. But this does not change the fundamental principle that every discussion has a theological and existential basis which is presupposed even when it is itself being discussed, and that the partner in the discussion may determine his own presuppositions, provided only that he expresses them clearly and communicates them to the other partner.

The dogma of the Church is the presupposition of any intra-ecclesial dialogue between the Church and the theologian. True, one may reject this dogma and refuse to talk to the Church in these circumstances. But without it an intra-ecclesial dialogue is impossible, because there would be no truly independent partner. For in this case a person would want to conduct a Christian theological dialogue while arrogating to himself the right to determine what is Christian. But this would mean a monologue, or else a dialogue such as exists (or should exist) among all men, and which presupposes no definable foundations. So the outcome is either a Christian monologue or a merely human dialogue. Hence an ecclesial theology presupposes the acceptance of the dogma of the Church, and a true dialogue with a partner independent of oneself exists only when the Church is allowed to determine what she retains as her dogma. This, however, is not meant to deny that this dialogue must be concerned with the Church's dogma itself. For this is situated in history, in which it always receives new forms and must be restated according to the needs of the time, indeed, it retains its permanence only through this change, if it is not to degenerate into an unintelligible formula. As has been said before, one necessary form of this change is precisely the dialogue between the Church and the theologian as the representative of new questions and horizons in which the permanent dogma of the Church must appear. But, to say it once again: This dialogue is conducted in the hope of an ever new reconciliation between the individual and the collective consciousness;

nevertheless, it may easily be replaced by a theological monologue unless the theologian accepts the indisputable faith of the Church also as his own condition for this dialogue. True, he must always adapt the alien elements if they are to become his own faith, but he accepts them only if he has the courage to give them power over himself.

Perhaps I have spoken only of the old ecclesiality of theology, though my subject was the new one. But just this ancient ecclesiality seems always new to me, even in the sober and often dreary daily run of ecclesiastical theology. Despite all he sees and hears, the truly Catholic theologian will always experience the dependence of Catholic theology on the Church as the sheet-anchor outside his own subjectivity though grasped by it, which alone enables him to overcome that dangerous alienation through which one is imprisoned in one's own individuality. This cannot be understood by someone to whom his own opinion always seems to be more important and true than that of another or of a community, and who thinks that he can achieve the full development of his personality only in opposition to a community. But this attitude is not mine, nor is it the attitude of Catholic theology. Nor do I think that such an attitude has a genuine future. I know that one must be very careful about predicting what the future may hold. But I think nevertheless that the attitude I have sketched and which is incompatible with an ecclesial Catholic theology is only the last attack on the ecclesiality of theology; it is actually the attitude of a late European individualism which, in the longer view, is already moribund.

True, the Church must also defend a permanent element in modern individualism which has been gained by terrible suffering, namely freedom of conscience. This freedom must also be proclaimed when it turns against the Church, and this not only in a spirit of civil tolerance inflicted on the Church from outside, but through the Church's own understanding of herself. It seems that we are approaching a more highly socialized civilization which yet cannot be without a common ethos if it is not to degenerate into a materialistic technocracy. Now leaving the Church out of account for the moment, such a future society will be faced with the question how it can ask all its members to subscribe to such an ethos without replacing (or at least endangering) the freedom of the individual by an enforced ideology and indoctrination. It must further be asked how such a society can have a truth that makes free without leaving man in a void in which neither he nor society can live. This question will confront society when it has used up the traditional ethos. Indeed, ecclesial theology has always asked and tried to answer this question, at least when this theology has been personally responsible without emancipating itself from the Church and her faith. Future generations will again pose the question of truth as an element of society, hence the old question of the ecclesiality of Christian truth is still a new question.

Meditation on the Word "God"

What can be said about the word "God" in a short meditation is but a very brief introduction to this infinite theme.
Such a meditation is both meaningful and difficult. It is
difficult because one can ultimately meditate on a word
only by examining its meaning. True, a word has a reality
of its own, which is the concern of the various linguistic
sciences, but it reveals its essence only if we leave it itself
behind and approach what it signifies. If this is true, a
meditation on the *word* "God" will yet again become a
meditation on God himself, and this would certainly go
beyond the possibility and the aim of these considerations.
Nevertheless, we shall not be blamed if, by meditating on
the word "God", we shall time and again transcend its
limits and consider the reality it expresses.

Yet it seems to me that a meditation on the *word* "God"
is, indeed, meaningful. This is so not only because, in
contrast to many other experiences which can be realized
without a special word, in this case the word alone can
make real for us what it signifies. We shall come back to
this later on. But the consideration of God can and must
perhaps begin with the word for a much simpler reason.
For we have no experience of God as we have of a tree,
a man, or similar "external" realities. These, though never
actually without a naming word, require that such a word

be given them simply because they appear at a certain place and time. Hence it may be said that the simplest fact of the question of God is this, that man's spiritual existence contains the word "God". We cannot escape this simple fact by asking whether there might not be a future humanity in which the word "God" no longer occurs. In this case the question whether this word has a meaning and signifies an external reality either does not occur at all or else the word has no longer its original significance and must be replaced by a new word. At the moment, however, the word still exists. It is also always renewed by atheists who say that there is no God and that such a concept makes no sense, who build anti-God museums, make atheism a party dogma and invent all sorts of other things. Thus the atheists, too, contribute to the continued existence of the word "God". If they wanted to avoid this, they ought not only to hope that the word will one day disappear from the language of human society, they ought themselves to contribute to this disappearance by not mentioning it at all, not even calling themselves atheists. But how are they to do this if their partners in the dialogue from whose language they cannot separate themselves speak of God and are interested in this word?

The very existence of this word is worth considering. If we thus speak of God, we do not, of course, mean only the German or English word for "God". It does not matter if we say *Gott* in German or *Deus* in Latin, or *El* in the Semitic languages or *teotl* in Mexican and so forth, though it is, of course, a very obscure and difficult question how we can know that all these different words mean the same thing or person, for in this case we cannot simply point to a common experience of what is meant, independent of the term. But for the time being we will leave this problem alone.

There are, of course, proper names of God or gods, whether in the polytheistic religions or, as in ancient Israel, where the one omnipotent God, Yahweh, bears a special name because the people is convinced to have had a special experience of him in its history, which characterizes him despite his incomprehensibility and actual namelessness and thus confers a name on him. But of such names we do not want to speak.

The word "God" exists, and this by itself merits consideration. But the English word "God" (like the German *Gott*) says nothing about him. Whether this was so when the word was first used is another question. Today, at least, the word sounds like a proper name: what is meant by it must be known from another source. This is a fact, even though we are not usually aware of it. If, as happens in the history of religion, we were to call God Father, or Lord, or heavenly King or something like that, the word itself would convey a meaning through its well-known origin or secular use. But the mere word "God" says nothing about what is meant, nor is it a pointer to something outside it, as "tree" or "table" or "sun" is. Nevertheless, the very fact that this word is so indeterminate is well suited to its meaning, no matter whether it had originally been so or not. Today, at least, it reflects what it signifies: the Ineffable, the Nameless One, who is not part of the definable world, the Silent One that is always there yet always overlooked, and, because it says everything wholly and without multiplicity, can be passed over as meaningless. For it has really no word at all, because every word receives its own particular intelligible meaning only within a complex of other words. Thus the "blind" word "God" which appeals to no definite individual experience is just right to speak to us of God, because it is the last word before all is muted; because all definable

individuality disappears and we are faced with the one
who is the foundation of all.

The word "God" exists. Thus we return to the beginning,
to the simple fact that in the universe of words with which
we build our world and without which even the so-called
facts do not exist for us, the word "God", too, occurs.
Even for the atheists, even for those who say: God is dead,
God exists, at least as the God whom they declare dead
and whose ghost they must chase away, of whose return
they are afraid. They would be at rest only if the word
itself ceased to exist, that is if the question of God would
no longer have to be posed at all. Nevertheless, this word
is still there. Even Marx thought that atheism, too, would
have to disappear, so that the very word "God", whether
affirmed or denied, would occur no more at all. Is such a
future conceivable? Perhaps the question is meaningless,
because genuine future is that which is radically new,
which cannot be foreseen. Or the question seems to be
merely theoretical and immediately changes into a question
of our freedom, whether we shall also challenge one another in future by saying "God", be it affirming, denying
or doubting him. In any case, the believer sees only two
possibilities: the word will either disappear completely,
leaving no trace, or it will remain as a question for all men.

Let us consider these two possibilities. Supposing the
word "God" had disappeared without leaving any visible
gap and without being replaced by another word which
would have a similar effect on us, which would pose at
least the one fundamental question, even though we do not
want to give or hear this word as an answer. What will
happen if this hypothesis is to be taken seriously? Then
man will no longer be confronted with the one whole of
reality as such nor with the whole of his own existence.
For this is done only by the word "God", whatever its

phonetic form or origin. If the word "God" really did not exist, this twofold unity of reality and of human existence would no longer be there for man. He would forget himself completely, being wholly immersed in the details of his world and his existence. He would not even be confronted with the whole of the world and himself in silent confusion. He would no longer be aware of being only an individual, not Being itself; he would only ask questions, but not consider the basis of all questioning, he would only manipulate ever new single moments of his existence, but would never confront it as one whole. He would remain stuck within the world and himself, no longer able to think of himself as a unique whole and thus to transcend himself, entering the silent strangeness from which he now returns to himself and his world, differentiating and accepting both.

He would forget the whole and his own ground, and at the same time forget, so to speak, that he has forgotten. What would happen then? We can only say he would have ceased to be a man, he would have returned to the state of the animal. Today we can no longer so easily say that if a being on this earth walks erect, lights a fire and works on a stone, he must be a man. We can only say that he is a man if he thinks and speaks and freely questions the whole of the world and his existence, even if he cannot answer this one total question. Thus it might also be conceivable that humanity may die a collective death, continuing to exist biologically and technologically while changing back into a nation of incredibly clever termites. Whether this is a real possibility or not, the believer in God need not be frightened by this idea, for it does not contradict his faith. For he accepts a biological consciousness, an animal "intelligence" if we may call it such, which is not yet aware of the question of the whole.

For such a consciousness the word "God" has not yet become its destiny, and he will not easily venture to say what such a biological "intelligence" can achieve without being involved in the destiny signified by the word "God". But actually man exists only when he says "God", even only as a question answered in the negative. The absolute death of the word "God", wiping out even its past, would be the signal—though heard by none—that man himself has died. Such a collective death might be conceivable even despite a biological-rationalistic survival. It need not be more extraordinary than the individual death of sinful man. Where even the question had disappeared no answer would be necessary. But the very fact that the question of the death of the word "God" can be put shows that this word is still there because of man's very protest against it.

The second alternative is that the word "God" remains. Every man experiences his unique existence only through the language in which he lives, which he cannot escape. For he accepts its verbal relations, its perspectives and principles even when he protests and cooperates in its evolution. Language has still something to say to us, since we still speak through it even while protesting against it. Hence we must ultimately trust it, or else we shall either become completely dumb or contradict ourselves in the very act of speaking. This language in which we live responsibly contains the word "God". It is no accidental word which turns up at one time and disappears at another. For the word "God" questions the whole world of language in which reality presents itself to us. It asks what is the origin of reality, whilst the world of language contains a paradox, because it is both part of the world yet also its whole, because it is conscious. When speaking of something language also speaks of itself, pointing to its ground which is taken away from it, and by this very fact given: this is signified when we say "God" even though we do not mean by this the same as language as a whole, but the ground on which it rests. Precisely this is why "God" is not just any word, but the word, in which language—that is the self-statement of world and existence—apprehends itself in its ground. This word belongs to our language and thus to our world in a special and unique way, it is a reality in itself, moreover a reality which we cannot escape. This reality may be more or less obvious, it may speak to us more or less distinctly, but it is there, at least as a question.

In this context it does not matter how we react to this word-event, whether we accept it as pointing to God himself or reject it in desperate fury, because as part of the world of language it wants to force us, who are part of the world, to confront the whole of the world as well as ourselves without being the whole or being able to rule it. And at the moment we will leave it open how this original whole corresponds to the manifold world and the many words of language.

We would here only draw attention to one thing, because it is directly related to the word "God". What has so far been said about it does not mean that we first actively think the word "God" individually and that it thus invades our existence. No, we hear it passively; it meets us in the language in which we are caught up willy-nilly and which questions us as individuals without being itself in our power. Thus this history of language in which the word God which questions us occurs is once more an image and parable of what it announces. We must not think that the word "God" is our own creation only because its phonetic sound is produced by us. Rather the word creates us, because it makes human beings of us. For the true word "God" is not simply identical with the same word as found in the dictionary among a thousand other words. For this dictionary word is only a substitute, as it were, for the real word. This real word is present to us in the connection and unity of all individual words and confronts us with reality as a whole, at least as a question. This word is present in our history and indeed creates it. And because it is a word we may hear it, as Scripture says, with ears that hear but do not understand. Nevertheless, it is there. Tertullian's concept of the *anima naturaliter christiana,* i.e. the originally Christian soul, derives from this inescapable word "God". It has the same origin as man himself and it ends only in his death; it may still have a history which we cannot imagine, simply because it keeps open the free and unplanned future. This word opens an unfathomable mystery; it wears us out and may irritate us, because it disturbs our life which wants clarity and planning. It is always open to the objection of Wittgenstein who tells us to keep silence about what we cannot say clearly, but who violates this very maxim by pronouncing it. Properly understood the word itself agrees with this mystery, because it is itself the last word before the silent worship of the ineffable mystery, which does not, of course, mean that the end of all speech is to be followed by that death which turns man into an inventive animal or a damned sinner. If it were not to be heard as an all-transcending word, it would only be an everyday word among other words and would have nothing but the sound in common with the true word "God". There is a good *amor fati.* The proper translation of this "love of fate" is "love of the spoken word", that is of the *fatum* which is our destiny. Only this love of the necessary liberates our freedom. Ultimately this *fatum* is the word of God.

God is No Scientific Formula

It may be said that God is not present in the realm of science and in the world organized by it, that the scientific method is therefore *a priori* a-theistic, since it is concerned only with the functional relationships of the individual phenomena. The believer will not contradict this. For God may not be used as a stop-gap. For what happens in this sphere, that is, what can be proved experimentally, can certainly not be what we mean by God in the proper sense of the word.

God is not "something" beside other things that can be integrated into a common homogeneous system. If we say "God" we mean the whole, not indeed a sum of phenomena to be examined, but the whole in its incomprehensible and ineffable origin and ground which transcends that whole to which we and our experimental knowledge belong. This ground is meant by the word "God", the ground which is not the sum of individual realities but which confronts them freely and creatively without forming a "higher whole" with them. God is the silent mystery, absolute, unconditioned and incomprehensible. God is the infinitely distant horizon to which the understanding of individual realities, their interrelations and their manipulation must always point. This horizon continues to exist just as distantly even when all the understanding and action

relating to it have come to a standstill. God is the unconditioned, but conditioning ground, the sacred mystery
because of this everlasting incomprehensibility.

If we say "God" we must not imagine that everyone
understands this word and that the only question is whether
what all mean by it really exists. Very often the man in
the street believes it to mean something which he rightly
denies, because what he imagines it to mean really does not
exist. He thinks it is a hypothesis for explaining phenomena until science can give the true explanation, or
someone to frighten children until they realize that nothing
extraordinary happens if they are naughty. The true God
is the absolute, sacred mystery to which one can only point
in silent adoration. For he is the silent abyss and thus the
ground of the world and of our knowledge of it. He is
incomprehensible in principle, for even if we were to
discover a "world formula" it would not even explain
ourselves, and this formula, precisely because it was understood, would again be enveloped in the infinite mystery.

For the mystery is the only thing that is certain and that
goes without saying. It calls forth the movement which
examines whatever can be explained, but it is not gradually
exhausted by this movement which we call science; on the
contrary, it grows with the growth of our knowledge.
Hence we cannot imprison God in an exact formula, we
cannot assign a place to him in a system of coordinates.
We can only stammer of him and speak of him vaguely
and indirectly. But we ought not to be silent about him
only because we cannot speak of him properly. For he is
present in our existence. True, we may always miss him,
because there is no definite point which we might indicate
and say: There he is. Hence we may be told to be silent
about what cannot be expressed distinctly. But the believer
will, because of his own experience, understand a "wor-

ried" atheist who is silent before the dark secret of existence. Simone Weil's words, namely that a man who denies
God may be nearer to him than one who only speaks of
him in clichées, may well be applied also to many who call
themselves Christians. Such a man may be nearer to God
because of his unfulfilled metaphysical longing, that is if
he does not selfishly enjoy, but truly suffers it. For in this
case he knows more of God than the so-called believer
who regards God as a question which he has long settled
to his own satisfaction.

Nevertheless, God is there, not here or elsewhere, but
everywhere in secret: where the ground of all silently
confronts us, where we encounter the inescapable situation
of responsibility, where we faithfully do our duty without
reward, where we realize the blissful meaning of love,
where death is accepted in the midst of life, where joy no
longer has a name. In all such modes of his existence man
is involved in something other than the strictly definable.
Hence he must become more conscious of transcending
what is individually determined; he must accept this transcendence—perhaps against much resistance—and finally
courageously defend it. This speaking of God may ultimately only point to the question which is man himself
and thus hint at God's mystery in silence, the result may
be less adequate than any statement on another subject,
the answer, aimed at God's bright 'heaven', may ever
again fall back into the dark sphere of man or may consist
in inexorably upholding the question that transcends any
definition, formula or phenomenon. At least in such efforts,
whether successful or not, man continues to question, he
does not despair and he will receive an answer because
just this question is blessed with the experience of the
incomprehensibility which we call God.

If a man who has experienced this trusts that this in-

comprehensibility, ineffably close, communicates itself
protectingly and forgivingly, he can hardly be called a
mere "theist" any more. For such a man has already experienced the "personal" God, if he understands his "formula" correctly and does not imagine that God again
becomes merely a "good" man. For what this truly and
blessedly means is that God cannot be less than man,
endowed with personality, freedom und love, and that
the mystery itself is free protective love, not an "objective
order" which one can, after all, possess (at least in principle), and against which one could ensure oneself. Such a
man has already understood and actually accepted what
Christians call divine grace. The primeval event of Christianity has already taken place in the centre of existence,
namely the direct presence of God in man in the "Holy
Spirit". However, much must happen before this man will
become a Christian in the full, authentic sense of the word,
namely the encounter of this primeval Christian event
with its own historical appearance in Jesus Christ, in
whom the ineffable God is present to us also in history,
in the word, in the sacrament, and in the confessing community which we call the Church. But this necessary and
holy institutional Christianity only has a meaning and is
not ultimately a sublime idolatry if it really introduces
man to the trusting, loving surrender to the holy and
nameless mystery. This surrender is accomplished by freedom, which receives itself from this silent mystery, and
thus our answer comes from the "Word of God" itself.

Of course, man of our scientific age, brought up, as he
thinks, to sober exactness, will call such talk emotional,
mere poetry and cheap comfort. For it is no formula
according to which we ourselves experiment in order to
arrive at a palpable result. This talk babbles of the one
experiment of life which the mystery accomplishes in us.

And in every life, even in that of the scientist and technologist, there are moments which will draw him into the centre of existence, when infinity looks at and calls him, who is now one with the responsibility of existence itself. Will he then shrug his shoulders and look the other way? Will he only wait until he is "normal" again, that is, absorbed by his interest in research and his daily life? Perhaps one may often react in this way, making commonplace man who forgets himself over material things the measure of all things, even when he investigates the universe—but will such an escape always be successful? Will he then be quite honest with himself? Surely this flight may not really be caused by sober objectivity, and a man may even pretend to venerate the incomprehensible silence while his whole attitude actually remains an escape and he only wants a superficial and guilt-ridden well-being in order to escape from the claim of the incomprehensible. Could this escape succeed even when life no longer permits a man to pass on to research and the daily round? Perhaps he may even violate the ultimate dignity of both daily life and research because he refuses to let them reach into the sacred sphere of mystery which surrounds them. We can master life with scientific formulae insofar as one has to make one's way among various events, and this may be frequently successful. But man himself is grounded in an abyss which no formula can measure. We must have sufficient courage to experience this abyss as the holy mystery of love—then it may be called God.

God, Our Father

I thought it went without saying that "Father" was a basic theological concept, hence I looked up the word in the excellent *Handbuch theologischer Grundbegriffe* by H. Fries (Munich 1963). But the word has no entry of its own and is not even contained in the subject index. This may be only an accident, such as happens even to theologians, especially as the thing itself, of course, can be found under other headings. But it may also indicate an uncertainty as to whether we are still able to call God "Father".

The God of the philosophers is no "Father", but the incomprehensible ground of all reality which escapes every comprehensive notion because he is a radical mystery. This is always only the beyond, the inaccessibly distant horizon bounding the small sphere we are able to measure. He certainly exists for us also in this way, as the unanswered question that makes possible any answerable one, as the distance which makes room for our never-ending journey in thought and deed. But does this ineffable being which we call God exist only in this way? That is the question. True, the distance which philosophical theology establishes between God and ourselves is still necessary to prevent us from confusing God with our own idols, and thus it is perhaps more than philosophy, it is a hidden grace. But the question whether God is only unapproachable ineffability must be answered in the negative. He is more, and we realize this in the ultimate experience of our existence, when we accept it without rejecting or denying it under pretext of its being too good to be true. For there is the experience that the abyss protects, that pure silence is tender, that the distance is home and that the ultimate question brings its own answer, that the very mystery communicates itself as pure blessedness. And then we call the mystery whose customary cipher is "God"-Father. For what else are we to call it?

Much paternalism in our world has certainly tried to invest custom and inherited power with a glory designed to prevent us from bearing freedom and responsibility ourselves, as well as the loneliness resulting from both. We experience the technical achievements of this world not exactly as an expression of tender, fatherly feelings but rather as hard and inhuman. The pressure of life often prevents us from realizing what we mean by calling God Father, a concept distilled from our notions of human fatherhood. Nevertheless, if we are resolved to let God be God, if we adore him as an ineffable mystery, not to be inserted as a definable factor into the sum of our life, we may suddenly experience him as communicating himself, as merciful and forgiving, indeed, as grace, and thus call him Father; though mother, love or home would express this just as well, because they also describe a primeval experience, preserving the bliss of the secret hour.

"Father", however, is also a good word and suited to the world which is given to us and through which we must express him. For there will always be fathers in this world, and even today we experience them not only as exercising an irksome authority, but also as the power that supports us by sending us forth into our own life and liberty. Applied to God, the word "Father" signifies the origin

that is without origin, the ground that remains incomprehensible, because it can be comprehended only through
his grace that keeps us while we emerge from it. "Father"
means the serenely loving seriousness, the beginning that
is our future, the creative power that accomplishes its work
patiently and without haste, which does not fear our
desperate complaints and premature accusations. He sends
us his mystery, himself, not anything else as partial answers; he sends himself to us as love and thus answers the
question which we ourselves are, and thus reveals himself
as "Person", disposing of himself in full knowledge.

Such experience exists, and not only momentarily, but
always. It opens itself to us always new, in serene detach-
ment. Nevertheless, it is difficult to encounter this experience; for its opposite is quicker and imposes itself more
brutally. But we need not have this experience by ourselves, for in this respect, too, no man lives to himself
alone. Even our most intimate, unique experiences happen
in our life because they encounter similar ones in other
men, and thus meet themselves. The history in which we
live our common life together is the place where everyone
finds himself. Now there we may find a man who called
himself simply the Son and who said "Father" when he
expressed the mystery of his life. He spoke of the Father
when he saw the lilies of the field in their beauty, or when
his heart overflowed in prayer, when he thought of the
hunger and need of men and longed for the consummation
that ends all the transitoriness of this seemingly empty
and guilty existence. With touching tenderness he called
this dark, abysmal mystery, which he knew to be such,
Abba (which we ought almost to translate as "daddy").
And he called it thus not only when beauty and hope
helped him to overcome the incomprehensibility of existence in this world, but also when he met the darkness of

death and the cup in which was distilled all the guilt, vanity and emptiness of this world was placed at his lips and he could only repeat the desperate words of the Psalmist: "My God, my God, why hast thou forsaken me!" But even then that other, all-embracing word was present to him, which sheltered even this forsakenness: "Father, into thy hands I commend my life."

Thus he has encouraged us to believe in him as the Son, to call the abyss of mystery Father, to realize both our origin and our future in this word alone, and thus to measure the dimensions of our dignity, of our task, of the danger and experience of our life. True, only the crucified is *the* Son. But he is also the sign that we all are truly children of God and dare and must call Father this true God himself, and not only the finite idols we ourselves imagine and create. Because he is the Son we are empowered to set aside the daily experience of the absurdity and torment of this life, to realize the true ground of this experience and to change it into an incomprehensible but blissful mystery by calling it Father. Can we say anything more improbable? But how else can we break through the mere semblance of truth, which we short-sighted "realists" regard as truth itself, and come to the authentic truth that makes us blessed? For may truth not redeem and save? That is the question which decides our life. Whoever opts for the blessed truth calls it "Father". And we may be allowed to hope, if a man thinks that, in order to remain true, he must opt for a deadly truth, he has nevertheless loved in his heart the blessedly protecting truth of the Father, because he has been faithful to the truth he thought bitter.

If we believe in the fatherly truth that makes free we must celebrate four festivals. First, that the Son has come, which is Christmas; second, that he said "Father" in the

abyss of absurdity, which is Good Friday; then, that he
arrived at God the Father with the whole reality of his
being, that is Easter; and finally, that he gave us the courage of his heart to repeat "Father" after him, which is
Pentecost.

Let us consider especially Christmas. It is the feast of
the Son who came from the Father, in whom God as the
Father is accessible in everyday history, and not only in
the inaccessible experience of the inner man if we repeat
the word "Father" after the Son.

So we will celebrate this feast. The message of faith
which comes in the word we hear opens by grace the eye
of inner experience so that it may dare to understand itself
and to accept the "sweet secret of its strangeness" as its
true meaning. God is really near us, he is where we are if
we have really—not only notionally—reached the authentic man who is open to God's infinity. If this is the case,
then God's descent into the flesh will explain to us the
secret and blessed meaning of the openness of our all-
transcending spirit and of our flesh that is penetrated by
death. The message which encourages us to believe in the
message of our own gracefilled heart says that God's distance is but the incomprehensibility of his all-penetrating
nearness. He is there tenderly, he is near, his love gently
touches the heart. He says: Do not fear. He is inside the
prison. We only think that he is not there because there
has never been a moment in our life when we did not have
him in the sweetness of his ineffable love as soon as we
began to seek him. He is there like the pure light which,
though everywhere, hides itself by making all other things
visible in the silent humility of its nature.

The incarnation of God means: Trust the nearness, because it is not void. Let go, then you will find; give up, and
you will be rich. The incarnation says in the words of his-

tory, not only with the words of longing: The infinite
mystery which silently surrounds you does not rush towards you so that you will flee from it into your own familiar little life until it overtakes and destroys you in death;
it is not only the judgment which orders your small world
from the distance and judges its guilty finiteness. It is
rather the promised beatitude. It can approach us without
destroying us, it can tenderly enter our heart without
breaking it asunder, it does not, like a crushing judgment,
dash from distant heavens into the small sphere of our
existence. No, it comes as grace saving us into its own freedom which it makes ours. It is not the source of the fear
of death but the promise of our own infinity.

If we are not bored by the message of the incarnation as
it is presented to us in helpless words from the pulpit, but
meet it with a longing heart hoping to confront the ultimate question of existence, then we shall be able to celebrate the feast of the advent of the Son in which the mystery we call God (often imagining that this word has explained the mystery) is truly protectively near, on earth
and in the flesh where we are. Then we may well call the
mystery Father. Then we may continue to say the most ancient and wide-spread prayer of all religions: Our Father
in heaven. It is never old, neither today nor tomorrow.
Then we can repeat with the Son: Our Father who art in
heaven. Then we can speak it also in the darkness of our
death which we share with the Son. We shall then confess
the most simple thing of our existence, to understand which
needs a brave heart and spirit; namely that God is not only
good in himself, but—though it could also have been different—that he has entered this world in all his glory as
love, as our own future and its last end. Then, if we are
ourselves good, that is, if we are full of fatherly love and
childlike trust, if we are so "silly" and so "naive" to risk

this, we shall be embraced and supported by the strength of the sacred secret of the world and of our own existence which we call God.

Ultimately only the man who believes in the holy origin can believe in a final salvation, only he can believe in an infinite future (for all else would merely be transitory and a beginning of death) for whom history starts with this infinite future that posits the beginning of history. Only if a man believes in a holy God will he believe in a blessed life to come. Only few dare to say that they regard such a future as a chimera. And these few protest against the absurdity of existence probably only because they, too, measure life by the standard that belongs to eternal life and which they, too, presuppose. Hence all might confess: I believe in God, the almighty Father. Though even then there would still be the problems which are bitter until the bitterness of death. But they would be mysteriously redeemed.

The Theology of Freedom

Shortage of space prevents us from giving a survey of the doctrine of freedom as it emerges from the history of dogma and theology, or to discuss in detail the theological statements about the nature of freedom which are found in Scripture, tradition and the pronouncements of the magisterium of the Church. It must suffice to summarize what evidently results on the subject from revelation.

Freedom in History

Man objectivates his ultimate and permanent character-istics in the course of his individual and collective history, though he exercises them in every one of his acts without actually realizing it. Hence the history of salvation and revelation, including the history of Christian theology, is also a history of man's reflection on himself as a free being. Hence man does not always know expressly and adequately what is true freedom, nor does he use this notion unchange-ably in his statements on revelation and theology as if it were complete and needed no further deepening. True, the average school theology often gives this impression, but actually it is not so. Of course, we cannot here present even briefly the history of the Greek-Western concept of free-dom.

First, freedom is seen as freedom from social, economic
and political compulsion; it is the opposite of slavery,
serfdom, etc. Hence it is a quality of the citizen of an independent polis who shares in the government of the state.
Later the concept becomes more individual, contemplative:
He is free who has *autopraxia,* that is who can do what he
wants. This freedom from being tied to powers who alien-
ate a man from himself is increasingly limited to an interiority within which a man can be himself. Thus, if he
recognizes this inviolable spiritual sphere as the centre of
his true humanity he will and can be free at least in
this part of his being. It is sometimes thought that a man
can become free also in those spheres that differ from this
sublime "I", and which are governed by such powers as
nature, the state and so forth, and that he can do this by
giving up opposition and regarding them as indifferent;
that he becomes free by detaching himself from them because he realizes that they are mere shadows and quite unimportant. One thing seems to be noteworthy: even the
true freedom of choice, that is the freedom which consists
not only in the absence of external compulsion but in the
fact that man must freely decide about himself, and which
is, therefore, a demand rather than "freedom" — this freedom becomes evident only in Christianity, because only
there each individual is eternally valid (in the personal
love between God and man) and hence must realize himself in perfect responsibility and thus in freedom.

If the history of revelation has reached its final eschatological phase with Jesus Christ, and if the absolute finality
of this world's eschatological phase is not only a mere fact,
because God will not reveal anything new, but is contained
in the very essence of this phase, because the appearance of
the God-man can be surpassed only by the direct vision of
God himself — then this quality of the revelation in Christ

must also apply to man as a free being. The freedom God always guarantees to man is the freedom of accepting absolutely the absolute mystery which we call God, in the sense that God is not just one among other objects of our neutral freedom of choice, but he who only becomes known to man in this absolute act of freedom and in whom alone the very essence of freedom is fully achieved.

The essence of freedom is certainly not to be understood as the mere possibility of choosing between a number of objects, one of which is God. For in this case he would have a special place among these objects only because of his own objective character, but not because of the very essence of freedom. According to St. Thomas freedom exists only because spirit exists as transcendence. Infinite transcendence to being as such, hence independence and indifference with regard to a definite finite object within the horizon of this absolute transcendence, this infinite transcendence exists only insofar as it envisages the original unity of being in every act that is concerned with a finite object and insofar as it is constantly open to its "Whither", which we call God. We speak of a Whither of the experience of transcendence not in order to express it in as complicated and involved a manner as possible, but for a twofold reason: If we were simply to say "God", we might mistakenly be thought to be speaking of God as an objectified notion, while here everything depends on the fact that God is already given through the transcendence, and precisely where something finite is the object of knowledge. In other words, because we mean God precisely insofar as he is "in-explicitly" known in something (*in quolibet cognoscitur*, as St. Thomas says) and not insofar as he is explicitly, but secondarily spoken of, we cannot simply say "God". If we called the Whither of transcendence its "object", this would equally well conjure up the misunderstanding that it was an "object" such as is given elsewhere in experience. It would suggest that we were not speaking of the Whither of the originally experienced transcendence itself, since the Whither would have been objectivated (categorized) by secondary reflection on this immediate transcendence.

Freedom is Possible only through God

Freedom does not first take on a theological character when God is explicitly objectivated in terms of the categories which apply to objects. It is theological by its very nature, since in every free act God is present, though not explicitly grasped, as its fundamental impulse and final goal. According to St. Thomas God is known in every object non-explicitly, but really; and this applies also to freedom. In every free act God is experienced non-explicitly, but truly; and what is meant by God is only experienced in this way, namely the Whither (incomprehensible by knowledge and will) of the one original transcendence of man, which consists in knowledge and love.

The Whither of transcendence cannot be disposed of, but is the infinite, mute disposal of us whenever we begin to dispose of anything by judging and subjecting it to the laws of our *a priori* reason. Hence the Whither of our transcendence is present in a mode of rejection and absence proper only to itself. It surrenders itself to us in the mode of denying itself, of silence, distance, incomprehensibility, and thus as very mystery. In order to see this more clearly we must, of course, consider that in our normal experience this Whither exists only as the possibility of comprehending finite things, hence that we are never allowed to contemplate it directly, at least not in our normal experience. It is given to us only in the Whither of transcendence it-

self; thus we avoid all "ontologism" according to which
God is what we know first, and in which we know everything else. For this Whither is not experienced in itself,
but is only contained together with the experience of subjective transcendence. Apart from this the Whither as
well as the transcendence itself is always given only as the
condition of the possibility of categorial knowledge, but
not by itself alone. For this reason the Whither of transcendence is there only in the mode of a distance that rejects. We can never approach or grasp it directly. It gives
itself only by silently pointing to something else, something finite as the object of direct regard.

Freedom towards God

It is a decisive element of the Christian idea of freedom
that it is not only dependent on God and refers to him as
the basis of the freedom of choice, but that it is also freedom before God. This would not be a particularly difficult proposition if God were only regarded as one reality
among others, as one of many objects of the freedom of
choice as a neutral faculty. But now this freedom concerns
its very basis, hence may be guilty of denying the condition of its own possibility in an act which nevertheless
affirms this very condition: and this is the extreme statement of the essence of creaturely freedom which leaves the
customary categorial indeterminism far behind. It is decisive for the Christian doctrine of freedom that it implies
the possibility of a Yes or No to its own horizon, indeed
that it is constituted by this very possibility. And this is so
primarily not where God is conceived in categorial notions,
but where he is given not absolutely, but in the transcendental experience as the condition of every personal activ-

ity directed to one's earthly surroundings. In this sense we encounter God everywhere radically as the actual question put to our freedom in all things of this world and, as Scripture tells us, above all in our neighbour.

The Paradox of Human Freedom

Why, then, is the transcendental horizon of freedom not only the condition of its possibility, but also its real "object"? For by definition this horizon is also the condition of a possible No to itself, hence it is inescapably affirmed by such a No, as the condition of the possibility of freedom, and even denied as a notional object in theoretical or practical atheism. This act of a freedom that denies God is thus the absolute contradiction, in which God is affirmed and denied simultaneously, and this ultimate absurdity is at the same time made relative in the temporal sphere, because it is necessarily objectivated and mediated in the finite material of our life. But the real possibility of such an absolute contradiction in freedom cannot be denied, though it is denied and doubted in vulgar everyday theology. This happens whenever it is said that the infinite God could regard a tiny aberration in the finite world as no more than just finite, and hence could not magnify it by an absolute prohibition and an infinite sanction, considering it as directed against the divine will as such. According to this view the will which such a sin would offend is the divinely willed finite reality, and if we assumed another offence over and above this we should wrongly place God's will like a categorial individual reality beside that which is finitely willed. Nevertheless freedom makes it possible to say No to God. Otherwise there would be no freedom of the subject. For the free act is the act of the subject be-

cause it is transcendence, while the individual things in the
world which we encounter in the horizon of transcendence
are not events within an untouched space, but the historical
concreteness of the encounter of the transcendence which
supports our subjectivity. If this is so, then the freedom
with regard to individual encounters is always also freedom
with regard to the horizon, the ground and abyss which
causes these encounters. Now the knowing subject cannot
be indifferent to the abyss with which it has to do, especially also when this Whither is not its explicit object;
hence it has the freedom to be inevitably concerned with
God himself even if this happens always within the sphere
of the concrete individual. In its origin, freedom is freedom
of saying Yes or No to God, and thus freedom of the subject to itself. Freedom would only be the indifferent freedom to this or that, the infinite repetition of the same or
the contrary (which is only a species of the same), a freedom of the eternal return of the same Ahasverus, if it were
not of necessity the final freedom of the subject to itself that
is freedom to God, though this truest "object" of freedom
might not be conscious in the individual free act.

Freedom and Grace

A second reflection will elucidate the last theological
ground of freedom as freedom towards God, even though
it can here be only just mentioned. Our historical transcendence depends on God's offer to communicate himself; for
our spiritual transcendence is never merely natural but always surrounded and carried by a dynamic of grace that
points towards God's nearness; in other words God is not
only present as the horizon of our transcendence that ever
refuses itself, but also offers himself as our direct posses-

sion in what we call deifying grace. Because this is so, freedom in its relation to its ground receives an immediacy to God through which it becomes most radically the power to say Yes or No to God as such. This happens in a way that is different from the formal concept of transcendence as the merely distant horizon of existence and cannot be derived from it.

Freedom for Salvation or Damnation

As has been said before, freedom in the Christian sense cannot be regarded as a neutral power to do this or that in an arbitrary sequence and in a temporal order which would be interrupted only from outside, but could continue indefinitely as far as freedom was concerned. No, freedom is by its very nature concerned with the freely achieved final end of the subject as such. For this is evidently what is meant by the Christian statements about man and his salvation or loss, when he must freely be responsible before God's judgment for himself and his whole life. Then he will hear the ever-valid sentence on his eternal destiny according to his works, pronounced by a judge who does not consider appearances but the free, innermost heart of the person. True, Scripture presupposes rather than enlarges on man's freedom of choice, and its explicit theme, especially in the New Testament, is the paradox that man's continuing responsible freedom is enslaved by the demonic powers of sin and death and even by the law, and that it must be freed to the love of the law by the grace of God.

Nevertheless, it cannot be doubted that in the Scriptures sinful as well as justified men are responsible for their life in the sight of God and thus also free, hence that freedom is a permanent constituent of man's nature. The true nature of freedom appears precisely in this, that in the Christian revelation it is the cause of both absolute salvation and absolute rejection by the final judgment of God. In the common experience of daily life freedom of choice may appear merely as a quality of individual human acts, for which man is accountable only because he has performed them without his decision being preceded by an interior state or an external situation and thus in this sense enforced. Such a concept of the freedom of choice atomizes it by attributing it exclusively to the individual human acts, held together only by the identity of their subject and the length of his life. Hence freedom would only be a freedom of individual acts, attributable to a neutral person capable of determining himself ever again as long as the external conditions exist. In the Christian view, however, man is, through his freedom, capable of determining as a whole and definitively; hence he does not only perform acts which may be morally qualified but are transitory and for which he is only legally or morally accountable. Through his free decision he is rather truly good or evil in the very ground of his being, and thus, in the Christian view, his final salvation or loss is already present, even though perhaps still hidden. Thus responsible freedom undergoes a tremendous change in depth.

Freedom as Self-Realization

Freedom is first of all "freedom of being". It is not merely a quality of an act such as it is sometimes performed, but a transcendental qualification of being human. If man is really meant to determine his final destiny, if this "eternity" is to be the act of his freedom, capable of making

him good or evil in the depth of his being and not only
accidentally, then freedom must first of all be freedom of
being. This means: man is concerned with his own being
which is always in relation to itself, which is subjectivity,
not merely nature, always person, not simply "being
there" but always "by and with himself". Nothing that
happens to this being occurs apart from his own "self-
relationship" but only through it, through his insight and
freedom. This means that if something happens to him
it becomes important for his subjective salvation only if
it is freely understood and accepted by a free subject in a
very special way. His "I" simply cannot be put aside, it
cannot be made objective, it can never be replaced or
explained by another, not even by its own reflective idea
of itself; it is authentic origin not dependent on another
and hence not to be derived from another. Its relation to
its divine origin must never be interpreted by causal and
functional relations of dependence, such as exist in the
realm of our categorial experience, in which origin does
not liberate, but binds and retains. Because of his freedom
of being man cannot be compared to anything else nor
adequately integrated into a system or subsumed under an
idea. In an authentic sense he is the untouchable and therefore also the lonely and unsheltered, responsible to himself, who can in no way be "absolved" of this solitary
self, who can never throw himself on to others. Primarily,
therefore, freedom is not concerned with this or that which
it might do or not do. Basically freedom is not the capacity
to choose any object or mode of conduct, but the freedom
of self-understanding, of saying Yes or No to oneself, the
possibility of deciding for or against oneself which corresponds to the knowing subjectivity of man. Freedom is
never a mere choice between individual objects, but it is
the self-realization of man who makes a choice, and only

within this freedom in which man is capable of realizing himself is he also free as regards the material of his self-realization. He can do or not do this or that with respect to his own inescapable self-realization. With this he is inescapably burdened, and though its material will be different, it is either a radical self-realization or self-refusal with regard to God.

Freedom—the Capacity of the Eternal

We have, however, to consider that this basic essence of freedom is realized in time. The total self-understanding and the radical self-expression, the *option fondamentale*, remain at first frequently empty and objectively unfulfilled. Not every free action achieves the same depth and thoroughness of self-commitment *(Selbstverfügung)*. Though every individual free act risks total self-commitment, it always surrenders itself into the whole of the one free act of the one finite human life, because every such act is performed within the horizon of existence whence it receives its weight and proportion. Thus the biblical and Augustinian concept of the heart, Kierkegaard's idea of subjectivity, Blondel's "action" and so forth indicate that there is a basic act of freedom which penetrates the whole of existence. True, this is actualized in the individual temporal, localized and motivated human act, but it cannot be identified with this in objective reflection, nor is it merely the moral sum of these acts. Nor is this fundamental act only the moral quality of the final free act before death. Man's concrete freedom in which he disposes of himself and achieves his own finality before God is the unity-in-difference between the formal *option fondamentale* and free individual human acts, a unity that is the concrete being of the free subject that has realized itself. We would emphasize again that here freedom is precisely not the possibility of always doing something else, of infinite revision, but the capacity for something absolutely final, because it is done in freedom. Freedom is the capacity for the eternal. Natural processes can always be revised and diverted, and are for this very reason indifferent. *The result of freedom is the true and lasting necessity.*

Freedom—the Capacity of Love

This self-perfecting of freedom into the eternal moment is its self-realization before God. For the freely attained salvation or damnation which in the gain or loss of God may not be understood as a mere external reaction of a judging or rewarding God; it is itself already done in freedom. If freedom is to achieve salvation or loss, that is the destiny of the whole man, it must involve him in all his intertwined relations of past and future. Freedom is always the self-realization of man making his choice with regard to this whole accomplishment before God. It is thus the capacity of the "heart", the capacity for love. What is the fundamental act of man, in which he can gather his whole nature and his whole life, which can embrace all that is man, bliss, despair, everyday life and hours of destiny, sin and redemption, past and future? The answer is not obvious, but it is true: the love of God alone is capable of embracing it all. It alone places a man before him without whom man would only be horribly conscious of a radical void and nothingness; it alone is capable of uniting all the manifold contradictory powers of man, because it directs them all to God. For only his unity and infinity can create in man that oneness which

unites the multiplicity of finite things without abolishing
it; love alone makes man forget himself (what a hell it
would be if we could not do this in the end!); it alone can
redeem even the darkest hours of the past, for it alone
finds the courage to believe in the mercy of the holy God.
It alone reserves nothing for itself and thus can dispose
also of the future (which otherwise man seeks to save,
because he is fearful of his finiteness, which must be treated
with care); it alone can love even this earth together with
God and thus integrate also all earthly love into the moment of eternity, and it alone will not fail in this, because
it loves him who has never been sorry for having risked
this earth of guilt, curse, death and vanity. The love of
God is the only total integration of human existence, and
we have understood its dignity and all-embracing great-
ness only if we sense that it must be the content of the
moment of temporal eternity *(zeitliche Ewigkeit)* and thus
also the content of that eternity which is born from it in
the presence of God himself.

The Risk of Love

This love is not an achievement which could be exactly
defined; it is what every man becomes when he realizes his
unique essence, something that is known only when it is
done. This is not to say that there is no general notion of
love, according to the general statement that man is obliged
to love God and that this is the fulfilment of the whole
divine law and all the commandments. For this principal
commandment obliges man precisely to love God with his
whole heart. And this heart, this innermost centre of his
person and thus of whatever else belongs to the individual,
is something unique; and what is risked and given in this

love is only known afterwards, when man has found himself and truly knows what and who he actually is. In this love, also, man is concerned with the adventure of his own, at first concealed, reality. He cannot estimate beforehand what is demanded of him; for he himself is demanded, he is risked in his concrete heart and life which are still before him as the unknown future and which reveal only afterwards what this heart is that had to be risked and spent in this life. In all other cases one can know what is demanded, one can estimate, compare and ask whether the risk is worth the gain. One can justify what has been done by the result which turns out to make sense. In the case of love this is impossible. For it justifies itself, but it is only truly itself when it has been perfectly achieved with all one's heart.

Love has No Measure

Fundamentally the Christian ethos is not the respect for the objective norms with which God has endowed reality. For all these are truly moral norms only where they express the structure of the person. All other structures of things are below man. He may change and transform them as much as he can, he is their master, not their servant. The only ultimate structure of the person which adequately expresses it is the basic power of love, and this is without measure. Therefore man, too, is without measure. Fundamentally all sin is only the refusal to entrust oneself to this measurelessness, it is the lesser love which, because it refuses to become greater, is no longer love. In order to know what is meant by this man needs, of course, the multiplicity of objective commandments. But whatever appears in this multiplicity is a partial beginning of love which itself has no norm by which it might be measured. One may speak of this "commandment" of love if one does not forget that this "law" does not command something, but asks of man to be himself, that is the possibility of love by receiving God's love in which God does not give something else, but himself.

But despite, no, because of his absoluteness God is no impersonal It, no unmoved receptacle of the transcendence and love of the spiritual person; he is the living God, and all human activity is essentially response to his call, which is the ultimate basis of its historicity. This historicity of man is taken seriously only when he knows himself to be essentially, not only accidentally, something that cannot be disposed of, but is integrated into the sovereign freedom of God. This is actually only the anthropological expression of the fact that every creature depends permanently on God. In the case of man this means that he remains dependent on God in his understanding of himself which is characteristic of his humanity, that he can never integrate God as an element into this understanding. It belongs to man's creatureliness that he experiences and affirms the mystery of God and his freedom. He therefore accepts the creaturely dependence which is proper to him if he does not imagine that he may finally dispose of himself, for example as "pure nature", but that he must wait for an historical interpretation by God himself.

Love of One's Neighbour

What had been said above of the interrelation between the transcendental and categorial exercise of freedom is realized in this historical interpretation. Human freedom is always freedom with regard to a categorial object and an inner-wordly Thou, even when it begins to be directly freedom before God. For even such an act of a direct Yes or No to God does not envisage immediately and solely the God of original transcendental experience and his presence as revealed in this, but first the God of thematic categorial reflection, the notional God.

If the word of God can be spoken in this world at all it can only be spoken as a finite word of man. And, conversely, the direct relation to God is necessarily mediated by inner-worldly communication. The transcendental message needs a categorial object, a support, as it were, in order not to lose itself in the void; it needs an innerworldly Thou. The original relation to God is the love of neighbour. If man becomes himself only through the love of God and must achieve this by a categorial action then, in the order of grace, the act of neighbourly love is the only categorial and original act in which man reaches the whole categorially given reality and thus experiences God directly, transcendentally and through grace.

In this relation to one's fellow men dialogical freedom enters history even more deeply, because it is concerned not only with the sovereign God, but also with the decisions of human beings, by which it is determined and which, in certain situations, it has to determine itself.

Thus freedom is always called to decisions which cannot be derived from general norms and eternal laws alone (even though they must not contradict them) and which nevertheless are not left to an arbitrary choice but claim the whole man because of his special call.

True, man's freedom is free self-realization towards achieving finality. Yet, despite its special creative character, it is a creaturely freedom. This is evident from two things. This freedom experiences itself as supported and authorized in its transcendental nature by its absolute horizon, which it does not form but by which it is formed. For neither in the knowledge nor in the freedom of love may the transcendental spirit be conceived as designing its goal itself. This reveals itself to the knowing and willing spirit rather in a peculiar remoteness; but, as has been said before, without that openness alleged by the ontologists. In the spiritual existence the goal is experienced as the actually moving cause. The spirit's own design for its future experiences itself as supported by the opening goal of which the spirit does not, however, dispose, but by which it is constituted in its being. The very transcendentality of freedom as supported and authorized by its goal signifies its creatureliness, which it experiences directly by exercising it. Insofar as this authorization of freedom towards absolute being is experienced as absolute nearness to this goal permitted by grace, the character of creaturely freedom becomes clearer when this goal opens itself, even though this experience can become objective only through its interpretation in supernatural revelation and in faith.

The creatureliness of freedom further shows itself also in this, that it is necessarily mediated by the surrounding world. Man always exercises his original freedom by passing through the history which is given to him. Freedom is a free Yes or No to necessity and thus once more experiences its creatureliness.

Creaturely freedom is conditioned by the situation; for it does not simply possess itself but it must first gain itself, and this it can do only in the encounter with other freedom, in the common life in the world. According to Christian doctrine the growth of freedom is always also determined by guilt. This is implied above all in the doctrines of original sin and concupiscence. These doctrines mean that man's freedom finds no situation or material for its own decision that have not already also been partly determined by the guilt of mankind, and till the end of history it will not be possible wholly to eliminate this burden of guilt.

Insofar as freedom always needs foreign material in order to find itself, it will always be alienated from itself. As has been shown before, it can never regard what it has done in a situation sufficiently clearly to know with absolute certainty whether it has said Yes or No to itself and to God. This is so because it can never be said with absolute certainty whether the objectivation in a certain situation springs purely from freedom and never from nature. Because this freedom is mediated by creatures it will always be ultimately equivocal and thus a mystery which must surrender itself to God. This equivocal character of the objectivations of freedom when reflecting on its original nature is increased by the fact that the material on which it must be exercised is always also determined and formed by the guilt at the beginning of the history of the spirit. Of course, the free individual can always either ratify the guilty determination of this material as an embodiment of his own No to God and thus turn it into an objective appearance of his own guilt, or he can overcome it in a Yes to God through his participation in the Cross of Christ. But just this equivocal meaning of the given situation turns the original free act once more into an insoluble mystery for freedom itself, leaving the meaning and quality of the individual life and of the history of mankind as a whole to the inscrutable judgment of God.

Inasmuch as freedom is always and in all its acts directed to the mystery of God himself, the act of freedom is essentially always the act of man's surrender to the providence of God and in this sense a trusting risk. It appears only slowly in history how God deals with this freedom which must entrust itself to him unconditionally unless it wants to refuse him. Even though, according to Catholic teaching, human freedom has not been destroyed by original sin, it has nevertheless been deeply wounded; hence, though God need not completely re-create it, it yet needs his loving help. Injured freedom must accept this help freely, yet it cannot do even this on its own initiative but needs the "prevenient grace" of God's unfathomable counsel, who "has mercy upon whomever he wills, and (who) hardens the heart of whomever he wills" (Rom 9:18) but of whom we must also believe that he "desires all men to be saved" (1 Tim 2:4).

Freedom is a mystery first of all because it is only from God and towards God, who is, however, himself essentially the incomprehensible mystery. The ground of freedom is the abyss of the mystery which can never be conceived as something not yet known but knowable in future, but which is the primeval fact of our transcendental knowledge and freedom. Moreover, in its permanent incomprehensibility it is the ground of all comprehension of the individual things we encounter within its horizon.

We cannot here pose the question of the real knowability of freedom in the theory of knowledge. Freedom does not belong to empirical psychology, for this can only state functional connections of individual data within the sphere of experience. Freedom, however, is always apprehended before such an objective experience as a transcendental experience in which the subject knows himself to be free.

Freedom is Subjectivity

This radical mystery of freedom continues in the free act of the subject as such. The individual free act participates in the mystery of its origin and goal insofar as its freedom and hence its moral quality is never absolutely objectifiable. This peculiarity results not only directly from the strict subjectivity of freedom, it is also explicitly emphasized in revelation. The above-mentioned total decision in which a man finally commits himself, that is in which he places his wholeness into its freely determined finality (and only then can an act be called completely free) must, according to revelation, be left only to the judgment of God. True, man produces his finality in freedom and as a conscious subject, but he cannot objectify this result of his freedom and its consciousness, that is, he cannot judge his own state, let alone that of others, before God. According to Catholic doctrine man cannot judge his justification or his eternal salvation with absolute certainty while he is still a pilgrim, and this is ultimately not contradicted by the Protestant doctrine of justification either, despite all controversies, because in Lutheranism, too, absolute "fiducial faith" has always been attacked. Thus a man cannot reflect on his free decision adequately and with complete certainty. Freedom is truly subjectivity, that is something more original than objects that can be unequivocally defined in an existing system of general notions. Freedom designs, as it were, its own system while exercising itself; man knows in the very act of his freedom who he freely is and wants to be. But this very knowledge is strictly himself, hence he cannot separate it from himself as a separate entity and thus once more say to himself what he freely says towards God. This statement which is himself disappears, as it were, into the mystery of God.

Freedom and Moral Judgment

An absolutely certain objective statement about a man's exercise of freedom in a certain definite act is impossible for

the man himself and even more for others. This is a principle. But it does not mean that freedom and responsibility cannot be found in human experience and relationships. Freedom is always exercised on given particular
material, even when it is total commitment of the free subject. Subjectivity is always accomplished in naturality
(Naturalität). This shows that human freedom is creaturely. It is also clear that though it is impossible for man
to reflect on himself adequately he is nevertheless a being
that objectivates himself and places himself under universally valid norms. It is Catholic and also biblical doctrine
that we cannot only evolve formal principles of subjective freedom regarding right and wrong, but also material,
objectively and universally valid norms for exercising subjective freedom in the categorial material of man and his
world. Thus it is a matter of course that man is both able
and obliged to judge his moral state objectively and to
arrive at a well-founded opinion about the way he uses his
freedom.

This possibility of self-knowledge and self-criticism
which can arrive at certain valid results is characterized
by man's existence as a pilgrim in this life, in which freedom is still active, hence every examination is itself a free
action which cannot be adequately examined. This knowledge gives a kind of certainty such as is possible in the
realm of history and freedom, that is as a claim to make
freedom itself a binding norm. Man has the right and the
duty to apply his knowledge of himself and others in the
decisions and actions of his life, because otherwise one cannot exist, and to abstain completely from such judgments
would not avoid the risks, but would itself be a free risk
and decision. Nevertheless this judging knowledge of freedom knows that it is not final, but subject to appeal. In
this objectified knowledge man accepts himself and sur-

renders himself to the mysterious judgment of God which takes place in the unreflected act of his freedom. Freedom is mystery.

Freedom through Christ

God has made known in his Son the irrevocable decision to set freedom free. Hence the history of freedom is salvation history. It is the experience realized in Jesus Christ that God has given himself to man's freedom in what we call deifying grace in absolute nearness and as the ground of the free acceptance of this nearness. God himself has given himself to the freedom that surrenders itself to him in his inmost divinity, he is not only the distant horizon to which man directs his free self-understanding, but has become the object of the exercise of this freedom in absolute immediacy. This exercise of freedom in Christ is what St. Paul calls the "freedom of the children of God", the truly Christian freedom. The love of the Father revealed in the Son made flesh (Jn 8:36), the *aletheia*, sets free (Jn 8:32), because where his *pneuma* is, there is freedom (2 Cor 3:17), since "for freedom Christ has set us free" (Gal 5:1). This freedom is freedom from sin (Rom 6:18–23; Jn 8:31–6), from the law (Rom 7:3f.; 8:2; Gal 2:4; 4:21–31; 5:1, 13) and from death (Rom 6:21f.; 8:21): from sin, insofar as this is the free self-assertion, in its innumerable variations, which is not open to the love of God; from the law, insofar as this becomes for the graceless man only the cause for asserting himself against or before God, even though the law is God's holy will and may be either broken or proudly fulfilled; from death, insofar as this is only the phenomenality of guilt. This freedom which is Christ and which he gives is appropriated by the man who obeys the call to this freedom in faith and through the baptism which is its expression, submitting himself to the event that opens the prison of the world; namely the incarnation, death and resurrection of the Son.

In this experience of freedom it has become clear that, as far as the whole history of man's freedom is concerned, man's No to God has been permitted only because God has communicated himself to the freedom of his creatures and thus, in the history of salvation, his Yes remains victorious. Man's freedom is freed into the immediacy of God's own freedom of being. It makes possible its highest act, of which its formal nature is capable, but which is not demanded of it. The freedom to and from God as the origin and future of freedom, and freedom as a dialogical power of love are accomplished in the highest modality of these aspects: as freedom supported in personal love by God's own self-communication and which accepts God himself, so that the horizon and the object of the love that is made free to itself become identical.

Origins of Freedom

It must first of all be clarified what freedom means theologically, and especially why it must always be conquered anew. We shall thus gain a proper understanding of the question why freedom must be conquered, and a deeper insight into the life of freedom.

Formal Characteristics of Christian Freedom

In Christian theology freedom is not simply a freedom of choosing between individual realities and objects encountered in our life, it is not merely the freedom to decide upon one course of action among others. Whether we know it or not, true freedom is born from the transcendence of man, hence it is freedom before and towards God. Even if God is not known or not expressly visualized in the free act: wherever freedom is really exercised, this happens in silently stretching beyond all individual data into the ineffable, quiet, incomprehensible infinity of the primeval unity of all thinkable reality, in an anticipation of God. Thus we experience precisely in freedom what is meant by God, even if we do not name or consider this ineffable, incomprehensible, infinite goal of freedom, which makes possible the distance to the object of our choice, the actual space of freedom. God is not one of the many realities with which we are concerned in the freedom of our affirmation or rejection, but originally he is the infinite horizon which alone makes the free choice of individual things possible. As such a horizon God is always encountered in the free act and is present in it. Thus freedom is necessarily freedom before God, even if he is not named, it is a Yes or No to God himself. Certainly, the free act is always also concerned with a finite object which one considers, which one desires, realizes, loves or rejects, destroys, hates and so forth. And in explicitly notional religious knowledge, in explicit religious action God, too, can, indeed must become one of the explicitly conceived individual objects of the freedom of choice, because in finite notional knowledge he is expressly conceived and thus, in a strange duplication, the horizon and condition of all knowledge is itself once more conceived within this horizon. But our freedom is not concerned with God only in this case. It is always concerned with him in Yes or No, wherever it is truly itself. For real freedom with respect to an individual object is possible only where transcendence in knowledge and deed is directed to that infinite and never attained goal which is the sphere of God. Wherever in absolute engagement—which no adult can avoid indefinitely—freedom takes up a position toward a definite finite truth, regardless of whether this position is correct or not, there the ineffable Whither of transcendence which we call God is affirmed or denied in the Yes or No to the ultimate possibility of freedom. Hence moral freedom is necessarily always also religious freedom; even if this is not expressly known, it is at least silently experienced in the fact that this freedom cannot be transmitted, in the responsibility and infinity of freedom. For the experience of freedom is inseparable from the experience of God; the exercise of freedom is always at least implicitly the decision between existential theism and atheism.

In this act of freedom man decides his own destiny. Of course, the one free act of man in which he realizes himself once and for all is dispersed in space and time in his many free actions, in which the one fundamental decision of the one man is enacted. As regards its content, the one free act of man in which he commits himself is either an act of loving communication with another "I", and thus with God, or the act of absolute egoism, which refuses the risk of lovingly entrusting himself to another. The essence of freedom consists in this absolute commitment of the subject. We do not everlastingly do this or that, we do not constantly react to ever-new objects and situations, but by doing what we do we make ourselves, once and for all, despite the temporal sequence. Freedom is not the capacity for indefinite revision, for always doing something different, but the one capacity that creates something final, something irrevocable and eternal, the capacity of what by itself is everlasting. Freedom alone creates that which is final. Certainly, this depends on the possibilities God has given to freedom, not only on the formal structure of freedom itself. But we know through Christian revelation that God has given himself as the absolute possibility and the absolute future in what we call grace, Holy Spirit, and justification. Hence the innermost essence of freedom is the possibility of absolute self-commitment to radical finality through the final acceptance or rejection of the self-communication of God himself, who thus becomes the horizon, object and subject of man's freedom. The one drama of God and man is enacted in our daily, free and personal life, and only because this drama takes place does freedom in a radical theological sense exist at all.

Grace and Freedom

This formal characterization of freedom does not prejudge and anticipate the Christian message of freedom. First of all, I do not think that today there is or should still be a controversy between the Christian Churches and denominations as to whether freedom exists in salvation and justification and whether the theology of man should or should not describe him as a free being. In my view there is at least today a distinct experience and teaching in Catholic theology according to which God must be understood as the all-efficient Giver who gives himself both the potency of freedom and its good act according to his grace that is neither derived nor compelled, and which nothing in man precedes. Hence all specious sharing out of divine and human causality in this matter is false and an heretical attack on the absolute sovereignty of God. Even in the Catholic, and not only in the Protestant view of the relation between God and man the freedom of the latter as derived only from himself is guilty and imprisoned egoism; hence as far as he is concerned, this freedom refuses to accept God's self-communication and to let God be God. Hence God's grace, which ultimately means himself, must set freedom free for God. It can therefore perform its very own deed to which it is called, namely to receive God from God through God, only in this way, and thus all truth of man as a free being proclaims either this liberation of freedom by God or the freedom by which man becomes guilty before God. Thus the theological doctrine of freedom proclaims the grace of God, while the "natural" freedom of man in potency and act is only the presupposition, created by God himself, to make it possible for him to give himself to man in love. Thus understood, the doctrine of freedom need not be a point of controversy between the denominations. This doctrine of freedom can pass over the question whether it is described as a property of the "natural" essence of man or emerges only through the call of God, who reveals and communicates himself as love. For, on the one hand, this interpretation of freedom is historically possible only in the specifically Christian view of man as it has developed through the Gospel message. On the other hand, it says of man what he always is, because he is always called by God and, through the offer of grace, is confronted with the absolute question even when he has not yet received the historical word of the Gospel. If we finally say that man experiences what is meant by God precisely while exercising his responsible freedom we do not mean that the *Deus absconditus* has thus already become the *Deus revelatus*. Under the secret call of grace in which God offers himself, this freedom is always meant either for judgment or salvation, and only the Gospel says reliably where this leap of freedom leads: it encounters the God of forgiving grace, indeed it is made possible only by him.

Freedom as Demand and Possibility

There are thus three aspects of freedom: freedom as deciding the relation to God, freedom as finality and freedom as final self-commitment, and these imply that freedom has to be realized. This sounds like a commonplace, but it is not. For man regards freedom mostly as an existing fact and thus fails to consider the question that freedom is something that has to be realized, and as such is not a fact, but a demand. Hence men are inclined to regard freedom as indeed the cause of certain things, but which has a meaning only with regard to the deed it performs. They are greatly tempted to value only the objective results of human action and the objective human states, regardless of whether they have come into being with or without freedom. Only too easily will the free act appear to them as the origin indifferent in itself of an objective state which might have originated in principle just as well without freedom and must be valued only for what it is. But if freedom is the final self-realization of the subject before God and if this self-realization, this eternity of man, can happen only in freedom, if the eternity of the creature is but the fruit of freedom and its own finality, then freedom is that which has to be realized. Then there are objective finalities which have to be realized but cannot except in freedom; then the final act of freedom, which also translates time into eternity, is the only thing that is radically subjective, because it is irreversible and irrevocable. Then the eternally valid can be realized only through freedom. And this makes freedom as possibility and as deed the only ultimate objectivity which has to be realized. God's eternity which he bestows becomes really my own when it is accepted by freedom and thus becomes man-made eternity. True, the free act by which God's self-communication is accepted is itself the gift of God and can only be realized as grace. Nevertheless, God gives and can give himself only by giving us the act of our own freedom which accepts him. Hence grace happens essentially and can exist only as the deliverance of freedom towards God. This is not the place to show that this concept of freedom either exists explicitly in the creed of the Church or is implied by the teaching of Christianity, that free faith justifies, that salvation must be received from God in freedom and that the eternity of salvation is not an indefinite continuation of time but must be understood as the final result of history itself which is produced by freedom.

The Corporeal Nature of Freedom and its Sphere

Before speaking of the existence of freedom and in freedom something will have to be said about the specifically
human creatureliness of freedom which will clarify the
dialectical character of our relation to our own and other
people's freedom.

Every human action is connected with some materiality.
Space and time constitute the external atmosphere in which
the free human act is accomplished. For the body and soul
of man are not two realities which have subsequently been
united, but two constituents of one and the same human
being which cannot be reduced to each other. They are not
two separate beings, but two metaphysically different
constituents of the one human being. The body is the exterior of the so-called soul and thus the act of the soul
translated into the exterior.

Hence our freedom is bodily freedom, and this means it
is realized as the original self-determination of a personal
subject in space and time. It must be furnished with such
material in which it must express and embody itself. Subjective freedom can only be realized in objects that are not
identical with it. It aims at foreign objects; when the subject realizes itself it changes that which is different from
itself; when the free subject returns to itself it enters the
sphere of the other in order to find itself. Even the innermost act is still external, because it belongs also to the
physiological sphere which is open to external influences.
Hence a perfect interiority of freedom is impossible. The
external element is necessarily part of the self-realization
of freedom. This sphere of foreign bodies is at the same
time the one open space in which subjects communicate
with other subjects and with the world. Despite its original
subjectivity freedom is realized in the common sphere of

the unity of historical subjects. By realizing my own freedom I also partly determine the sphere of the freedom of
others. True, I do not change their freedom, but the sphere
in which their freedom is realized, hence this affects the
possibilities of their subjective freedom. Freedom is always
realized in a concrete sphere. Persons who realize their
freedom are not the untouchable Monads envisaged by
Leibniz. Every free act of one person changes the objective
possibilities of the free act of his neighbour, it enlarges,
changes or limits the sphere of the other's freedom before
this latter can freely intervene. Hence the realization of
freedom is a concrete problem of human relations. True,
there is an absolute freedom, but no absolute sphere of
freedom, for this would amount to the solipsistic denial
of other free subjects. But this freedom which is realized in
the social sphere must contain a moral demand to be respected by others. Hence the relation of many freedoms
within a common sphere is, both individually and col-
lectively, historically variable. Because of its objective
embodiment every free act produces a change in the sphere
of freedom shared by all, hence this sphere is in constant
historical motion, it is, as it were, always distributed anew.
Therefore the distribution of this sphere will always give
rise to controversy. The question whether revolution can
be justified would have to be discussed in this context. True,
every man will have his own personal section of freedom
within its one whole sphere, but the size and character of
this personal section are in constant flux and cannot be
defined once and for all. Hence we cannot decide *a priori*
the question how this common sphere of freedom can best
be divided so that the freedom of each individual as well
as of the whole community is preserved. What once did not
belong to the material of freedom might well be part of it
today as well as the other way round. There is no authority

in the whole world which could plan the division of this sphere autonomously and for ever. This is so because the acting subjects are necessarily many, if for no other reason because even in the most totalitarian system there would have to be at least one subject which does the planning and cannot be planned himself. Hence the unplanned change in the sphere of freedom always takes place in the factual decision and contains the elements of unreflected spontaneity.

For this reason the Christian's historical action in society, State and Church bears inevitably the character of the risk, of uncertainty, of walking in the dark. For we know not what to ask, we must beg for gracious guidance from above, beyond what can be calculated and foreseen. If, because of this risk, a Christian thinks himself dispensed of taking individual decisions he sins against the historicity of his existence and becomes all the more guilty. For he must not only proclaim the ever-valid principles but also risk the concrete future, trusting to God. As a Christian, too, he must not only suffer but act, without the correctness and success of his action being guaranteed by the correctness of his principles. This is generally valid, but especially as regards freedom and compulsion and their concrete adjustment. The Christian must not only have the courage to represent a balanced eternal doctrine, but also to enunciate a contemporary slogan which he may, in certain circumstances, do in the name of Christianity, even though it cannot be pronounced by the official Church.

Thus it can be understood what the existence of (and in) freedom ultimately means. The theologian cannot analyze concrete dangers and duties connected with the handling of this one sphere of freedom by individuals and groups of men. Some theoretical considerations must suffice; but it is to be hoped that these, too, will be practically useful.

The Change in the Sphere of Freedom

In the history of the last centuries the sphere of freedom of
the individual has both been enlarged and also become
more threatened, because man himself can actively change
it. It has been enlarged especially by the technological
achievement of the present civilization and by the immensely enlarged possibilities at man's disposal. It has also
been enlarged by the emancipation of the sexes, by religious and civic tolerance and freedom, by the increasing
abolition of rigid social structures and taboos, in short, by
what we call a pluralist social order. At the same time this
sphere of freedom exists often only in appearance, because
all these achievements and social conditions inevitably
define this sphere of freedom in a very special way. They
do this without the free decision of the individual, and
thus this sphere of freedom does not remain empty, but
contains a definite choice of objects from which man may
choose in an always finite decision. This sphere of freedom
is threatened and secretly determined by anonymous
powers determining public opinion without being controlled themselves, which produce mass psychoses, direct
consumption and the ever more intricate relations of social
life. Thus both the enlargement and the narrowing of the
sphere of freedom are strangely interdependent, because
such things as technology, automation and the development of social relations which enlarge the sphere of freedom at the same time also furnish the means to restrict it.

The Christian's Yes to the Enlarged Sphere of Freedom

In accordance with his theology of freedom the Christian
will have, in principle, a positive attitude to the enlarged

sphere of freedom. By its very nature freedom needs an uncluttered sphere in which to realize itself, even if this implies inevitably the possibility and danger of a guilty perversion of freedom. Hence, if freedom is to be, because it alone makes possible finality and eternity, there must also be a sphere of freedom despite all danger. The subjective exercise of freedom is the demand of what ought to be. Where subjective freedom is only regarded as a possible way of producing objective reality, subjective freedom will be justified only by its object. In the nineteenth century Catholic theologians often assumed that subjective freedom was only a neutral possibility to do something, without possessing a moral claim in itself. From this it followed quite easily that only truth and goodness have rights, but not error and evil, which, on the contrary, must be prevented.

It cannot be the duty of individuals or society to take away the sphere of freedom, even in the case of wrong decisions, from other human beings. This would always be an attack on the dignity of the person and his freedom, which is not a means to an end (in this case the compulsory realization of something good), but part of the meaning and goal of the human person.

Any enlargement of this—though somewhat dangerous—sphere of freedom increases the chance of producing freedom. If, therefore, this sphere is enlarged, even though not without human guilt, this should not, on principle, frighten the Christian. If this sphere has become larger and inevitably more dangerous he may quite happily accept it as allowed by the Lord of history. He may admit that, relatively to all human civilization and society, there was formerly perhaps more that was specifically Christian in the world. But an outwardly homogeneous Christian society as the given sphere of freedom does not necessarily imply and guarantee that the Christian ethos is really realized in faith, hope and love and thus really produces eternity. It may also happen that such a Christianity gives the impression of a kind of drill, almost of a subtle form of brainwashing, a sociological routine which may produce a bourgeois Christianity but not Christian freedom, and which therefore remains unimportant in the sight of God. From the Christian point of view a pluralistic society may, indeed, be dangerous and harm the stock of Christianity and the Church. But God alone can know whether he may not produce from this as much fruit of freely achieved eternity as in the good old days of a united Christendom; he has not told us anything about it. However that may be, we Christians have every reason to regard the enlargement of the sphere of freedom through modern developments first of all as a positive chance for Christian existence, for as free children of God we can realize the grace of freedom that generates eternal salvation only in the freedom also of the natural spirit.

A Christian theology of freedom can regard any determination or limitation of the sphere of freedom only either as an inevitable consequence of the exercise of freedom by others, or as a provisional educational measure for the protection of a still maturing freedom. In the second case the aim will be to train man for making free decisions so that he will not be enslaved by powers which manipulate this space of freedom in such a way that moral freedom can no longer make its proper decisions within this sphere.

Freedom consists first of all in the courage to accept its larger sphere despite its danger. As it is given by God it is the divinely willed chance to exercise our freedom in it. This enlargement of the social sphere of freedom is actually of Christian origin and hence not actually suspect to Christians. True, throughout the history of Christianity and of

the Church the Christians themselves had slowly to learn—
and this process is not yet finished—what their Christianity really means; they must ask this question again and
again and answer it in ever new situations which they can
not, of course, foresee and for which they will not have
ready-made answers.

Thus Christians have not always been tolerant and
freedom-minded. They have persecuted each other and
non-Christians, often committing dreadful atrocities, and
they have often canonized forms of society that were
anything but free. We may mention, for example, the
principle *cuius regio, eius religio*, Leo X's bull *Exsurge
Domine*, directed against Luther, which condemned the
view that it was a sin against the Holy Spirit to burn here-
tics, or the ideology of the completely ecclesiastical state.
But even though this may be admitted and regretted, it
must nevertheless be realized that much in the behaviour
of Christians was not due to Christianity but to social
conditions which had not been created by Christianity
and actually blocked Christian possibilities and horizons.
Moreover, much of it, even though contradicting the ultimate logic of Christianity, originated as a claim to absolute
validity inherent in every great historical concept of the
world such as is still only too evident in militant communism.

Nevertheless, it ought at last to be stated that the passion
for social and cultural freedom is principally a Christian
passion, even though Christians often had to learn it from
those who had abandoned Christianity. For civic freedom,
after all, originated in the toleration of the various Christian denominations. Freedom was first and most radically
proclaimed as the freedom of faith and its confession. The
dignity of the individual person is a Western experience
grounded in the Christian knowledge of man as a child

of God and his eternal value as such. Let us ask quite simply: Would the inviolable dignity of every man continue to be acknowledged if it did no longer receive its force—even secretly—from this fundamental conviction? If man is regarded merely as a material or social factor, why should he not be used for any purpose, without his dignity being respected or even known? I certainly do not mean that only Christians respect this intangible dignity of the unique individual. What I say is that this respect is adequately understood only in Christianity and that it is actually of Christian origin.

For this reason it behoves Christians above all to respect not only the freedom of belief but freedom in itself. Otherwise Christianity would betray itself. We Christians must not be interested in freedom only in so far as it affects our own religious or even ecclesial purposes. For freedom is truly indivisible. German Catholics as well as Protestants ought to admit that under the Nazis their official representatives did not realize this sufficiently to defend the freedom of others. For the best proof of one's devotion to freedom is the readiness to grant it also to others. At this point the seemingly merely human concept of freedom receives a strangely Christian character and depth. For if we are really concerned for the freedom of others, we shall be prepared to give up part of our own freedom. We shall make this sacrifice, appearing as weak and stupid, incapable of defending ourselves, as men who give without receiving anything in return. This is the attitude of the Sermon on the Mount and of him who could freely have saved his life, but surrendered it to the guilty freedom of others even unto death.

Freedom and its Limits

This, however, is only one, even if the most important, aspect of the problem. For we would not be Christian realists but harmless and at the same time dangerous utopians if we were to imagine that Christians must practise an unrestricted liberalism. There is certainly a reasonable liberalism which has actually sprung from the Christian conception of freedom and the person, and this can well be a legitimate contemporary Christian attitude to society. Such liberalism may, in the past, also have represented the justified interests of an ultimately Christian-inspired social order against an over-conservative Church. We ought not to deny this, however unpleasant such facts especially of the last centuries of church history may appear to be. But there is also a utopian liberalism, a blind hatred of all social order, an irrational fear of anything that sets limits to individual caprice. Such social libertinism says freedom and tolerance while what is meant even if perhaps unconsciously, is arbitrariness and licence. We may mention in passing that such liberalism is actually very old-fashioned. The highly complicated society of the future will undoubtedly enforce ties and restrictions compared with which individualistic liberalism will appear as an anachronism. As Christians we represent personalism, but not libertinistic individualism, hence we have no reason belatedly to grow all enthusiastic over such an individualism in order to be modern. We may well join authentic non-Christian liberals in trying to make future social conditions as tolerable as possible, while avoiding the totalitarian dictatorship of classical communism such as is still practised today. But in view of the genuine ideals of communism we need not pretend that the Christian idea is antiquated, according to which a certain restriction and even compulsion are necessary for guaranteeing the greatest possible freedom to the greatest number.

For such liberalism forgets the basic fact that the enlargement of the sphere of freedom for one means inevitably its limitation for one or many others. Hence the true, indeed the only real problem of freedom in society does not consist in this, that an individual or an organized community unjustly deprives someone of a measure of freedom which it might well accord him, but that it must distribute the one finite sphere of freedom in such a way that all receive their due.

The true problem consists in this that the demand for a larger sphere of freedom itself inevitably threatens the freedom of others because it implies a diminished sphere of their freedom. Hence the very essence and realization of freedom in the life of the community involves legitimate limitations. These may take various forms, for example protection against unjustified interference, educational measures and compulsory assistance in communal concerns. A one-sided liberalism refuses to admit these; it pretends that its fight for freedom is only meant to liberate men from their fetters. In fact, however, the freedom publicly to propagate a certain idea, for example, inevitably narrows my own sphere of freedom provided only that I am freely opposed to this propaganda and that I am undoubtedly myself changed by this propaganda in as much as the preconditions of my personal decision are themselves altered by it. If I unwillingly have to see and hear a thousand times that a certain detergent is the best I am actually no longer as free to buy another as I should be without this advertising campaign.

The unlimited freedom of everybody to claim absolute freedom for everything works like a sort of secret brainwashing by anonymous powers which does not necessarily abolish freedom but narrows in advance the sphere in which the individual can make his free decision. And this happens inevitably wherever someone claims a sphere of freedom for himself. Whether it knows and wants it or not, individualistic liberalism is the implicit denial of the sphere of freedom of others. For it behaves as if I were involved with the free decision of another only when I make the same decision, but not before. But this is a capital error. We need only examine the furious protests against government measures so often heard today. The demands may often be quite justified or at least the object of rational discussion. But it is a capital error if such protesters argue, as often happens, according to the principle that I can personally do as I like, hence I should also let others do as they like, for if the other person does what he likes I can no longer do the same and act from the same situation which would obtain if the other had not acted. To this may be added the odd fact that the same people who claim to be defenders of freedom want to forbid Christians, for example, to send their children to denominational schools or to live according to their own moral principles.

Thus there is a legitimate (and in itself higher) principle of freedom and also a legitimate (though in itself lower) principle of justified compulsion, and these two principles cannot be simply assigned to separate spheres of human existence and action so that they could never come into conflict with each other. Hence we have the problem of correctly distributing freedom and compulsion within the one sphere of freedom. This distribution cannot be made once and for all, not even by revelation, because it depends on concrete situations. Thus man has the moral and Christian duty again and again to redistribute freedom and compulsion correctly, so that his dignity may be preserved.

This delimitation must take place within the framework

of general principles, but its performance will also always be unique and creative, because in it the dignity of freedom is most perfectly realized.

Freedom as the Courage of Commitment

We have now to find a concrete pattern according to which the one sphere of freedom for all men may be fashioned. A Christian social policy in favour of freedom cannot simply consist in advocating freedom and tolerance while trying to abolish all compulsory ordering of social life and public opinion because these are felt to threaten freedom. If we really want freedom in the Christian sense, that is, the largest possible sphere of freedom for all men, we must also have the courage to affirm the need for commitment, even for compulsion and for the authority that limits the freedom of individuals for the sake of others, and we must not be disturbed by the clamour of those who say that we are intolerant and suppress freedom. Power and authority which determine the sphere of freedom without the free assent of the individual are indeed dangerous and only too often become depraved by the guilty selfishness of those in command, but they are not by their very nature immoral opponents of freedom. The legitimacy of power can be doubted only by those who regard even the establishment of objective laws as sinful. Not everyone has a right to everything. And if in certain circumstances such a right is denied him, this is by no means necessarily an attack on his freedom, even though he may protest. The common good which limits the freedom of the individual is only another's right to freedom, so that the sphere of freedom is limited for the sake of freedom itself, and not by an alien element.

A completely free and detailed agreement about the concrete distribution of the sphere of freedom among all its subjects will never be possible, even though a voluntary agreement appealing to everybody's reason must be attempted. This is the obligation of all, and especially of all Christian authorities. Hence the life of society can never be completely without an element of struggle and compulsion, of an authoritarian decision which is also justified. Such a "free", unplannable interplay of authoritarian forces of society within the sphere of freedom will always exist; there will always be victors and vanquished. If a single institutional power were to claim to represent all authority absolutely and thus to guarantee all true freedom, this would already be a totalitarian system and a tyranny. But for this very reason a certain pluralistic antagonism among the powers that determine the one sphere of freedom cannot be avoided, indeed it is itself a guarantee of freedom, while on the other hand the governing powers cannot legitimately be asked to refrain from any interference in the sphere of freedom. This means that a distribution of the sphere of freedom which would always be acceptable to all is impossible; a permanently stable social system is a utopia. The Christian knows this, because he realizes that he will always live within the sphere of historical change. According to Catholic ecclesiology at least, the Church is not only a spiritual community, but a society living within the structures of time and space, hence she claims to have a share in the determination of the social sphere of freedom. Nevertheless, the Church as such may on no account appeal to the secular power to help her realize her own ends and to assist her special mission. She must not seek such assistance, especially not today, nor does she need it. But as members of society and of the state Christians have the duty to cooperate in the formation and distribution of the one sphere of freedom in a way that is suited to the object and to the special historical situation, and to realize that this is impossible without a responsibly and morally applied authority.

Freedom and the Demands of the Time

The actual shaping and distribution of the one sphere of freedom must, indeed, respect general principles of theology and the natural law, but cannot be deduced from them alone. For it always belongs also to creative historical decision; it needs courage and the realization of what is needed at a certain moment of history. Hence it is the task of individual Christians and of Christian associations to work out an historically effective image of the sphere of freedom.

Such an image ought not to appear antiquated and reactionary. Not all ancient laws and customs are worth defending. There are, indeed, certain Christian taboos which ought to be abolished and which we should not defend only because they once protected a freedom that had not yet come of age. In certain cases we may also safeguard our own freedom by a tolerance for others which goes farther than the nature of freedom demands. In our pluralistic society we cannot expect and not even wish that only that which corresponds to the natural law should be realized. We have the right and the duty to allow freedom to others also where we can foresee that it will be abused and where we might even be able to prevent such an abuse. Such a right and such a duty derive from the nature of freedom as well as from a proper interest in our own freedom. Today they are certainly much greater than in former times, when a pluralistic society such as we have now did not and could not exist. Undoubtedly the Churches are still making stupid mistakes in order to defend their own way of life and their own freedom by means that seem to deny their respect for the freedom of others, or which give the impression that we advocate freedom only where we do not have the power to keep it for ourselves.

There are, however, social controls which are always necessary to defend the freedom of all, even if they have to be upheld by force against individuals or groups which protest against them. This applies not only to the protection of the rules of democracy, because, on the one hand, even the laws of a democratic society may be regarded by some as an unjustified limitation of their freedom, and, on the other, there may also be laws which wrongly restrict freedom even though they were promulgated according to the rules of democracy.

Material regulations, too, belong to those social structures that may be compulsory in order to safeguard the freedom of all. We have the right and the duty to defend them, despite the protest of some. But we must know exactly what we choose to defend, so that the compulsory rules may protect the freedom of as many people as possible and we may not appear as straitlaced governesses of those who want to preserve their own freedom. The attitude of Christians is not so simple as that of the man who has a phobia of any authority, a fear which will ultimately lead to anarchy and the destruction of true freedom. But neither does the Christian favour a society with hard and fast rules so that there is as little freedom as possible to come to wrong decisions. In order to protect true freedom the Christian must always find a new relation to the dialectical unity between the largest possible sphere of freedom on the one hand and its perhaps compulsory distribution on the other. This relation cannot be adequately derived from the principles of Christianity or the natural law alone. In order to find it we must always make historical decisions, for it is an art of the possible, the combination of a mysterious inspiration from above with a constantly renewed examination of the present situation. But precisely for this reason all Christians do not only receive a complete and supposedly concrete natural law which is communicated to them by the official representatives of the Church, they also find out for themselves the actual requirements of public life, so that all may have as much freedom as possible, a freedom that can act with God in view and thus create that personal finality which receives God himself as its eternal meaning.

The Test of Christian Freedom

Christian freedom means human freedom, granted by God to every man as a dignity, a task and an inescapable burden. By the grace of God this human freedom is delivered from man's selfish isolation so that it can enter into the infinite, self-communicating mystery of existence which we call God. It is a freedom which only finds itself wholly in the light of the Gospel, founded on God in faith, hope and love, and thus realizes its own truth in the love of the neighbour and of God. But it is not yet clear what human freedom is as such. This we would not here state directly, but perhaps we may at least draw a conclusion about it from what will be said on the more detailed questions.

First of all: The free acceptance of the condition of a finite human being is essential to the adequate realization of human freedom. The will to the necessary is part of freedom. Freedom itself is also, if we may say so, *amor fati*, provided that the *fatum* (what is promised), which is met with love is understood to be promised by the God who is love, even, and especially, where he casts us inexorably into his incomprehensibility. Where freedom understands itself correctly, accepts and realizes itself such as it is, the necessary is not its external limit against which it hurts itself and fails, but that element in itself through which it finds itself as a freedom which can ultimately fail itself only through itself. Freedom is ultimately not the possibility of protest, but the possibility to change what is foreign into oneself, the possibility of acceptance and, insofar as it is not directed to an object but to a person, love. Freedom protests only where it understands itself and it destroys barriers only where they prevent it from being the capacity of acceptance and love, which assimilates itself to what is foreign as well as the other way round. Human freedom is finite, it can be exercised only through the nature of man, the physical and historical situation, the Thou as its horizon and material. However much it may be creative commitment even with regard to God and physical, biological and social self-manipulation of man, tending into an infinite and unknown future, when it is realized there remains always an alien element which it must either accept in hope and love or against which it must protest and thus lose itself, without being able to pretend that this seemingly heroic failure is its true fulfilment.

We have of necessity said this in a very abstract way, but it must be seen very clearly, especially today. For we are living in a world that has become dynamic and is manipulated by man himself, who, through his scientific and technological achievements, has freed himself to a formerly inconceivable degree from the compulsions of nature and from his own self-alienation, and this means that man has come to understand himself and to be his own property and burden. Yet despite all his new freedom he again enters the alien sphere of technology and of the immensely increased compulsions of institutions, of planning and organization.

But if all this is borne only protestingly as external compulsion then everything will be just the same as formerly or worse; for only the material of the fetters would have

changed, they themselves would have remained. Freedom
will find itself and its true nature only if the needs of
modern man, the highly socialized state, the many new
ties, the integration into the community are freely accepted, ultimately for the love of men and in the hope of
the infinite breadth of eternal life. But all this is even today
the free act of the individual, for which he must be trained
and formed, to which he may not, indeed can not, be
compelled. Today a training for freedom is necessarily a
training for love which patiently accepts those restrictions
without which the many who are to be loved can no longer
exist today. Where stubborn rebellion is not simply the
instinctive reaction of a caged animal fettered by social
ties, it may often be something like the almost inevitable
practice of freedom, the subject's acceptance of its own
responsibility. Such rebellion may also be the liberation
from the unjust restrictions which an ancient society with
fossilized traditions has fashioned for itself. Nevertheless,
rebellion is not the last word of freedom, it is not its most
mature form, especially not if it is in the deepest sense
unsocial, hence both old-fashioned and loveless.

Secondly, genuine freedom is the will to truth, because
this frees every man from those interior dangers which
threaten freedom more than all external restrictions, the
dangers of one's own shortsightedness, of pride and a
blinding egoism. St. John says: "The truth will make you
free", free for that freedom which one does not simply
possess, which might be threatened only by others, but the
freedom which every man must seek and for which he
must struggle. Certainly, there must be the freedom of
thought and the freedom to express one's conviction also
in public. This freedom accepts the risks inherent in it
convinced of truth's own strength and not afraid that such
expression of opinion might lead to chaos. This is certainly

one form of freedom; but it loses its own nature if it is understood merely as caprice which may utter any opinion; if the free individual is lacking in self-criticism and not brave enough to let himself be taught, to listen to the arguments of others and to look for objective standards. It is not right to claim for ourselves freedom of opinion if we want only to air foolish subjective views and half-truths without taking any notice of a knowledge acquired by hard work, of human experience and of genuine authority; though we must allow freedom of expression even to such people as long as they do not prevent others from voicing their opinion, thus destroying the freedom they claim for themselves.

Today this must be emphasized also with regard to the Church. The Second Vatican Council has rightly allowed much freedom of theological discussion within the Catholic Church. Post-conciliar theology makes it clear that many new questions still await an answer, that many opinions in both dogmatic and moral theology must again be discussed and even revised, including matters which are important for the Christian life. But this does not mean that suddenly everything has become problematic and a subject of individual opinion, that the Church has turned into an open debating society. True, it goes without saying that if a man cannot in conscience accept the doctrine of the Church as the norm of his faith, this must be respected by others, whether they think his view right or not; and the Church, too, must respect such a conviction and may not suppress it by social pressures or prevent its expression. It also goes without saying that only by the free assent of faith can one be a believing Christian, a Catholic. But if someone believes that he cannot and should not accept the authority of the Gospel, of Scripture and of the teaching office of the Church he cannot consider himself a Catholic, he cannot be a partner in the dialogue that takes place within the Church and which presupposes the acceptance of her teaching office in as far as it claims to have authority. We shall certainly carry on a dialogue with a person who thinks in this way with the same love and respect we show to separated Christians and others. But such a person should be honest and show clearly that he is not a Catholic in the sense that the Church understands the term. He ought not to attempt to introduce and spread un-Catholic opinions as tenable within the Church. Where it is doubtful whether a religious, moral or theological opinion is compatible with the official teaching of the Church (and such cases are possible), such an opinion may be a subject of discussion within the Church. But not everything is questionable. The creeds and the defined truths of faith, even those of most recent times, are not subjects of free discussion within the Church, nor have they become such through Vatican II. But neither wild avantgardists nor frightened traditionalists ought to pretend that now everything has become uncertain and everything that had been safe and clear has disappeared in the fog of doubt. An official doctrine of the Church does not lose its binding authority only because some theologian expresses—whether in a book, an essay, a lecture, on the radio or in television—an opinion of which another Catholic cannot understand how it is compatible with the doctrine of the Church; and mostly the theologian in question will not have tried very hard to show how it can agree with it. We may even say today that an imprimatur is no sufficient guarantee for the acceptability of an opinion. The mature Catholic must be cautious and critical also with regard to the utterances of Catholic theologians. Above all he must always realize that the freedom of a Catholic presupposes the acceptance of the Church's faith and an obligation towards her doctrinal authority. This is for him an internal principle of his thought because he has assented to it in a freely accepted faith. This authority does not limit his freedom, but frees him from the prison of his own subjectivity. If today some Catholics no longer want to learn from the Church that truth, and hence authentic freedom, too, is involved with society and therefore with institution, they should at least learn it from Marxist anthropology. They should also learn that the truth of the individual does not triumph when it breaks off the dialogue and withdraws into the splendid isolation of its subjectivity, but when it refuses to stop the dialogue with the truth of society, in this case of the Church, and freely lets itself be integrated into this truth.

Further: Christian freedom respects the freedom of others and is therefore tolerant, seeking the open dialogue with all men. Finite human freedom can be realized only in something objective, even if this were to be thought of as consisting merely in brain cells, conceptual mechanisms, associations, that is, basically in social or psychological models of thought, or if it were to belong—but only seemingly—to a merely inner realm of thought. This necessary objectification of freedom exists because this objectivation, as opposed to original personal freedom, can be produced also without freedom, from ordinary compulsion of all kinds to the sophisticated forms of brainwashing that are practised in the East as well as in the West.

This objectivation of freedom is also socially relevant, even where we seem to be concerned only with the innermost mind. For just this reason men may produce and enforce this objectivation of freedom without freedom, they are tempted to narrow or even destroy the freedom of others by such objectivation. But for the Christian it is decisive how this objectivation originates. It is not enough

for him that somebody has a certain opinion, or performs
a certain rite, which might be produced also without freedom by means of training, brainwashing, social pressures
and so forth. It is decisive for the Christian that this objectivation comes to pass precisely through freedom, for
only in this way will doctrine, rites, etc., truly belong to the
free person who realizes himself before God, either towards or against him, and thus becomes the person who
will be able to work out either his salvation or his eternal
loss. Everything objective in doctrine, worship, ecclesial
society and so forth is relevant to salvation only if it happens as an objectivation of freedom, is freely received as
such into the sphere of original freedom or serves such freedom, if it is original faith, hope and love.

If Christianity were to produce religious reality or its
counterfeit only through psychological indoctrination,
social pressure etc., it would ignore its own nature and
not create what it wanted, even if the outcome would
be very successful. Christianity can never come into being
through absolute social domination even if this were to call
itself Church and succeeded in influencing all men completely from outside. In order to bring forth true Christians the Church itself must will and create that sphere of
freedom which must necessarily also be the sphere in which
men can decide against Christianity. This is not merely a
concession, a toleration of the inevitable, it is not merely
Western liberal humanism; it belongs to Christianity as
such. Christianity is certainly not so unwordly as to turn
man into an absolute subject of pure interior freedom. It
knows that there are favourable and unfavourable conditions for the realization of freedom. Hence Christians mistrust those groups who arrogate freedom to themselves
and, under the pretext of freedom, would like to narrow or
abolish the sphere of Christian existence. The Church is

well aware of her own great and small sins in this respect; for in her desire for her own freedom she has narrowed the sphere of freedom, thus contradicting her own true vocation. She also knows that the concrete social formation of the sphere of freedom not only for Christians, but for all men, is a difficult task which must always be performed anew, also by the Church, and which depends on innumerable historical data.

But all this must not be allowed to obscure the decisive factor: The Church herself must will a sphere of freedom for all men, because without it free human beings and also Christians cannot exist. In this sense "tolerance" is not tactics, but an essential demand of the Church because without it she cannot achieve her end, namely the free self-realization of man, who entrusts himself to God, the ultimate mystery of his existence in faith, hope and love, a God who wants to give himself to man as his fulfilment and his absolute future in forgiveness and sanctification. Such freedom, however, is realized only if the sphere of freedom is conceded also to others even if their decision should be a wrong one. It can never be the task of the Church or of an authentic Christianity to prevent what is wrong at any price, even the price of freedom. We Christians ought to be the first to make the cause of the freedom of others our own and to be as sensitive to a threat against another's freedom as to one against our own. But if this be so we also have the right to vindicate the sphere of our own freedom, which is not confined to the church building and the sacristy, but which includes also public and social life. And if we Christians are many and hence cannot avoid to claim a considerable place in public life, then this is no illegitimate restriction of the freedom of others who are perhaps fewer in number.

What has been said means in practice that we Christians

must seek the dialogue with others, if only because the one social sphere must also be the sphere of the freedom of all men, which compels us to communicate with all men so that there may be a place for all. But beyond this the will to give freedom to all men signifies something deeper: The original free decision of all in the will of love, in the unconditional respect for others and so forth may be the same also if the free persons express themselves in contrasting objectivations. Different groups may not only have the same formal freedom, but also the ultimate correct attitude and decision in favour of that genuine goodness which is valid before God, even if this is differently interpreted. In controversies and disputes a profound common element may yet effect a reconciliation, namely the devotion to responsible freedom, the unconditional respect for the dignity of all men, the love of one's neighbour as well as of those who are farthest from us. Such an attitude contains implicitly and germinally the essentials of Christianity, namely faith, hope and love of God. This remains true even if on the one hand such people contradict each other in their original notional self-understanding, and, on the other, if the Church as the incarnational and social presence of God's grace can never give up the effort to let the uniting forces in their heart and conscience also appear in their profession of the one creed of the one Church. Hence the Christian who wills the freedom of all must also believe that the others are capable of dialogue. If he does not believe this he would have to regard them as condemned by God, which the Gospel forbids him to do. Hence the freedom of the Christian is, in the last resort, bound to be the holy foolishness which is the true wisdom of God; he must believe that the other wills the good even where, according to the Christian view, this will is realized in a wrong and threatening way. He must always grant to the other the chance of an open dialogue, because he can never ultimately say that there is no common ground for it. He must always place his hope in the heart which God alone can judge. Thus the Church and her members can carry on a dialogue also with all those who are outside. This dialogue should be concerned not only with social, political, cultural and economic questions in order to build and develop a world that is worthy of men, but also with philosophical and religious problems. The Christian knows that a dialogue is valuable even if he must hold on to his Christian convictions with absolute commitment and cannot hope for unity in the foreseeable future. For even the absolute conviction of faith concerns a truth which the Christian can penetrate ever more deeply through such a dialogue with all men, and which he, too, can always learn to understand still better. This truth which all other truths reflect in shadows and images is the incomprehensibility of God and his love.

Freedom is also the courage to risk the unforeseeable future. The freedom of responsible decision certainly demands knowledge, objectivity, reflection, circumspection. It wills *something* and is responsible for what it knowingly wills, but not for what is absolutely unforeseeable and may happen as a result of what has been done. Nevertheless, freedom is the courage to risk the unforeseeable future. For it is possible only where the individual object that is to be willed or realized is situated in the infinite transcendentality of the personal spirit, that is where it is seized in an anticipation of the absolute good. Further, freedom with regard to a certain object is ultimately the freedom of the subject to commit himself. Thus its transcendence is not only the condition of free action, but also that which freedom must ultimately accept and which it must confess. Thus freedom is the will to the un-

limited, to what cannot be surveyed, it is the freedom of
creative hope that accepts itself, anticipating what has
never yet been realized. Hence freedom is never only the
free repetition of what is already there, it is no endless
copying of the same models in a neutral space and time.
Nor is it the obedient respect for the law as for that which
commands always the same. Finite freedom, too, is creative freedom in authentic history, prepared for new things
which are both one's own and unexpected and unplanned
and only experienced in the hopeful journey into an open
future. If the absolute future of freedom is God, who is
also before and not only above us, then this God is precisely he who opens up the future to us as authentic history
which must be approached in a spirit of venture and hope,
but not calculatingly.

All this applies also to the Church. For she is the pilgrim
people of God which makes its way through history in
freedom. Her faith is her hope; her truth and her law of
love do not form a fence around something that is always
the same and need only be repeated, but they open up an
infinite future. Christians may never stop, they may never
set up anything as an idol, until the infinity of ineffable love
reveals itself and God himself confronts them face to face.
Today the Church presents herself as such a pilgrim of
hope not only in the silent hearts of her members, but also
in her empirical history. This corresponds to her nature
such as it must show itself when the world in which she
exists moves ever more quickly, being no longer our stable
home but becoming the womb of the future. Hence today
even in the Church much more is called in question than
in the recent past, changes are made much more quickly,
and instead of venerable customs we meet much that is new
and even questionable. True, this may partly be caused by
the human desire for novelty and perhaps rebellion, but

ultimately such social and empirical changes reveal the true nature of the Church as advancing hopefully into an unknown future. Thus the Church remains what she is and always has been, the people that has no abiding city here on earth, the pilgrim seeking the eternal home which is realized through this very pilgrimage because it has still to be built. Hence it would be a pusillanimous faith which believed that the Church must stand like a solid tower on the shore rather than meet her Lord walking on the waves of time. Her constancy in the risk of her historical freedom is guaranteed by her Lord, by her Spirit, not by something man himself has subjected for his use. We must train ourselves to trust *this* Church and to risk with her the free plunge into the unforeseen historical future. True, for such a pilgrimage into the future we shall need prudence, the will to historical continuity, planning of what can be planned (but only of this!), sober obedience to the government of the Church, distinction as far as possible between what is ever-valid and what is changeable in her faith and constitution, consideration for those St. Paul calls the weak and for the Church as a whole as well as patience with her human side. Above all, however, we need the courage to face the uncertainty of history without a false desire for security.

Lastly, realized freedom is the unique event of the personal uniqueness of every man in his finality before God. Here we touch the ultimate mystery of freedom in the Christian sense. Freedom is not the possibility of always doing something else and so also the opposite, it is not the motor of the eternal return of the same or the movement into the void. Despite its dispersal and extension in space and time freedom as act is the final commitment of the spiritual subject, event of eternity in time before God, acceptance or rejection of him who is incomprehensible love. Freedom is

not meant to pass the time but to gain eternity, because
God is made present through the Yes of freedom, regardless of whether this free act knows it or not. God enters
man's life out of pure grace because he gives himself freely
and because he gives freedom as potency and also as act
of his acceptance. But in this grace he delivers freedom
from man's self-absorption and leads it to his own incomprehensible glory. This ultimate nature of freedom constitutes the highest dignity of man and the foundation of an
authentic humanism. True, the dignity of man which
distinguishes him from an inventive animal and a mere
product of surrounding nature, this dignity may also be
attained and silently affirmed in the unreflected act of freedom selflessly performed in absolute responsibility. Nevertheless, this dignity is fully itself only if it is conceived as
the dignity of the being that creates itself into the final
perfection before God. Thus this being achieves an indestructible result which is worth preserving, because his
life becomes for ever the deed that accepts eternal life of
God himself. This happens wherever a man knows that he
is not a mere episode of nature, a transitory experiment
and a being that can lose itself in the empty past.

Humanism, therefore, is not a certain Western way of
life with all its historical limitations, which is gradually
destroyed by the hard technological age of man in the
mass, which rejects any self-important personality cult. In
the Christian view humanism is the unconditional respect
for every individual man. In its material content all concrete humanism is relative and conditioned by the age.
Christianity itself is not tied to any such concrete humanism. But in every historical human condition the eternal
dignity of man ought to be admitted, and all should have
the chance of realizing the ultimate nature of freedom,
that is, the action of eternity in time. And thus it is again

clear that the Christian Church can discuss with all men how true humanity is to be realized in time. For Christianity is not the same as a certain humanism, not even the humanism it has itself created in the West. It is rather the confession of the absolute future of man which is God himself. For this reason it is not tied to any concrete humanism. Hence it can discuss without preconceived ideas what is to be done so that man may freely become the event of eternity in time and that his secular activities may remain compatible with his eternal task and destiny.

Christianity is essentially freedom, and Christian education is training for freedom. But freedom has only understood and realized itself when it accepts God and the neighbour in him. But we know what God is and who our neighbour is only if we know freedom and have accepted it. Both together are the blessed and fearful mystery of life which is risked as love in faith and hope.

What is the relation between fate and freedom? This was and still is one of the great questions of mankind. In all such questions we are always aware of two facts but cannot understand how they are to be combined. Hence we are always tempted to deny, or at least to weaken, one in favour of the other. But true philosophy and theology must admit both—in our case fate and freedom—and to have the courage to remain open for both in our experience as well as in our theory. In such cases the Christian faith does not, indeed, enable us to understand how fate and freedom can be one and yet different; such understanding is denied to finite man. But it will give us courage and humility to accept both and to integrate their uncomprehended unity into that infinite mystery which we call God.

Fate or destiny, that which is destined for us, exists in a twofold sense. First through our direct experience: our life is a single chain of causes and their inevitable effects which are independent of our freedom and responsibility. If we reflect on this chain we can never point to one of its links and say with absolute certainty: this is due only to my free and responsible decision. For it may also always be interior or external fate. But neither can we ever say of the same link that it is only fate coming from outside. For whatever we thus encounter in our life is also in its entire reality partly effected by our responsible freedom. It is thus an insoluble unity of passive and active elements, of action and reaction, of fate and free self-determination. For we have no standard by which to judge what in this unity is our responsibility and what is *mere* destiny for which God is responsible. Such judgment is reserved to God alone. But if a man believes in the omnipotent, omniscient and loving God his life will be destiny in an even deeper sense: for it is wholly borne by the power of God without which nothing, not even man's own free act, can exist; his life as a whole and in all its details is always lived before the omniscient God of love. But it is supported and known by this God as precisely this unity of fate and freedom within which his own divine power has placed us. For God's omnipotence can create a free responsible being without diminishing created freedom, because divine omnipotence and creaturely responsibility increase together.

Whether a man may know something of his destiny and whether this knowledge is true or not, the burden and dignity of his freedom will always be with him. He can and should accept his life as far as it is inescapable destiny in faith and hope as coming from infinite love, even if this love is incomprehensible. Only thus will this destiny receive its true meaning and character even if, seen from outside, everything seems to be the same, whether we trustingly accept it or violently protest against the absurdity of life. Further, man is always under the obligation to use his freedom as much as possible for shaping his life; he may never abdicate his responsibility under pretext that everything happens in any case as it must happen. For the use or the refusal of this responsible freedom is precisely part of what "must happen". For if anybody had a sure knowledge of his future this very knowledge would either leave the space of his freedom still open and un-known, and would demand that he should take note of the situation of his freedom, or if the free decision were already included in the knowledge, this would be all the more a demand actually to make this decision.

SOURCES

I. RESPONSIBILITY IN THE POST-CONCILIAR CHURCH

The Christians' Responsibility for the Church after the Council:
Text of a lecture in Munich, 5 June 1966, first published in *Stellaner Nachrichten* 12, no. 8 (1966), pp. 3—14.

Advice to a Worried Catholic:
Text of a broadcast (North German and West German Radios), first published in *Oberrheinisches Pastoralblatt* 68, no. 5 (1967), pp. 129—32.

To an Impatient Catholic:
Text of a broadcast (North German and West German Radios), first published in *Oberrheinisches Pastoralblatt* 68 (1967), pp. 161—4.

Compulsory Alternatives:
Text of a broadcast, West German Radio, 4 December 1967.

Present Tasks:
Adapted version of "Blick in die Zukunft", published in N. Greinacher and H. T. Risse, eds., *Bilanz des deutschen Katholizismus* (1966), pp. 487—508.

II. CHRISTIAN FAITH — THE DELIVERANCE OF THE WORLD

Faith and Culture:
Text of a broadcast, South-West German Radio, 11 June 1967.

The Christian Character of the Secularized Ethos:
First published under the title "Das eigene Zeugnis" in *Spektrum*, supplement of *Presse*, Vienna, 24/25 December 1966, p. 3.

III. RELIGIOUS PATTERNS

Is Christianity an Absolute Religion?:
Orientierung 29, no. 16 (1965), pp. 176—8.

Visions:
Hitherto unpublished.

Medical Ethics:
Fortschritte der Medizin 85, no. 24 (21 December 1967), pp.
1029—30.

IV. ECUMENICAL PERSPECTIVES

The Question of Justification Today:
Text of a lecture in Soest i. W., 5 November 1967, on the occasion
of the 450th anniversary of the Reformation.

A Catholic Meditation on the Anniversary of the Reformation:
Stimmen der Zeit 180 (1967), pp. 228—35.

V. FREE ACCEPTANCE OF CREATURELINESS AND CROSS

"Remember, Man, that You are Dust":
Text of a sermon preached in Munich on Ash Wednesday 1967, first
published in *Geist und Leben* 40 (1967), pp. 1—3.

Passion of the Son of Man:
Text of sermons broadcast on the Bavarian Radio during Holy
Week (20—25 March) 1967.

VI. COMMITMENT TO THE CHURCH AND PERSONAL FREEDOM

Institutional Spirituality of the Church and Personal Piety:
Abridged version of a lecture to lay theology students of the
University of Munich, 31 January 1967, first published in *Christo-*
phorus 13, no. 1 (1968), pp. 23—28.

The Prayer of the Individual and the Liturgy of the Church:
First published in H. Schlier, E. von Severns, J. Sudbrack and A.
Pereira, eds., *Strukturen christlicher Existenz: Beiträge zur Erneue-*
rung des geistlichen Lebens (*Festgabe* in honour of Fritz Wulf SJ)
(1968), pp. 189—98.

Democracy in the Church?:
  Text of a lecture in Freiburg im Breisgau, 3 May 1968, first published
  in *Stimmen der Zeit* 182 (1968), pp. 1—15.

Theology's New Relation to the Church:
  Text of a lecture in Münster, 14 May 1968, first published in *Geist
  und Leben* 41 (1968), pp. 205—16.

VII. THE LITTLE WORD "GOD"

Meditation on the Word "God":
  Text of a broadcast on the South German Radio, 3 March 1968.

God is No Scientific Formula:
  Text of a contribution which appeared in several West German
  newspapers on 24 December 1965 and part of which was used in a
  lecture in Munich on 14 December 1966.

God, Our Father:
  Christmas supplement of *Presse,* Vienna, 24 December 1964.

VIII. TRUE FREEDOM

The Theology of Freedom:
  First published in O. B. Roegele, ed., *Die Freiheit des Westens* (1967),
  pp. 11—40.

Origins of Freedom:
  Text of a lecture to the *Evangelischer Kirchentag,* Cologne, 29 July
  1965, first published in M. Horkheimer, K. Rahner and C. F. von
  Weizsäcker, *Über die Freiheit* (1965), pp. 27—49.

The Test of Christian Freedom:
  Text of a lecture at the annual meeting of the *Katholische Erzieher-
  gemeinschaft* of Hessen in Frankfurt, 14 January 1967.

Fate and Freedom:
  Based on a radio interview on the problem of astrology, Bavarian
  Radio, 1 March 1967.